NEW-GENERATIONS

AFRICAN A

POETS A CHAPBOOK B
BOX SET A

AN INTRODUCTION IN TWO MOVEMENTS BY
KWAME DAWES & CHRIS ABANI

With special thanks to Martha Mattia
for her extremely generous contribution
to the success of this box set series

Published by Akashic Books
©2020 Kwame Dawes and Chris Abani

ISBN for full box set: 978-1-61775-816-4
Library of Congress Control Number for full box set: 2019943610

Akashic Books
Brooklyn, New York, USA
Twitter: @AkashicBooks
Facebook: AkashicBooks
E-mail: info@akashicbooks.com
Website: www.akashicbooks.com

African Poetry Book Fund
Prairie Schooner
University of Nebraska
110 Andrews Hall
Lincoln, Nebraska 68588

For Lorna,
Sena, Kekeli, and Akua,
Mama the Great,
and the tribe: Gwyneth, Kojo, Adjoa, Kojovi.
Remembering Aba and Neville.
K.D.

*

Remembering Daphne, Michael, and Greg,
and for Mark, Charles, Stella—my family.
I love you.
C.A.

NEW-GENERATION AFRICAN POETS (SABA)

Introduction by Kwame Dawes and Chris Abani

CONTENTS OF BOX SET

NEW-GENERATION AFRICAN POETS (SABA)

Introduction in Two Movements
by Kwame Dawes and Chris Abani

PART ONE

Sankofa

I will not be so bold as to make claims about directions and thematic trends in African poetry today because, after all, I come to this introduction not as someone who has attempted a deep scientific survey, but rather someone who, for the past decade, has been privileged to read a great deal of poetry written by emerging poets from Africa. And what I can say is that, as with generations of poets before them, this current generation is contending with what can best be termed "modernity" in African culture. And whereas in the past, notions of migration, globalism, and cultural "clashes" were defined by communication that was less fluid, less accessible, and more expensive, the fact is that the superficial "borders" that separate our worlds are more porous because we are traveling more, and we are connecting across all sorts of forms of media in unprecedented ways.

In reading this year's iteration of the *New-Generation African Poets Chapbook Box Set*, I kept being drawn back to the idea of border crossings, of movement, and, in many instances, of migration. Many other common threads of form and content emerge in this work, but I thought it would be fruitful to consider this core notion of movement—a phenomenon that Toni Morrison, in her long essay *The Origin of Others* (2017), declared to be the most dominant theme of the twenty-first century. These African poets are confirming this.

In Jamila Osman's poem "Winter," a drama unfolds—it is a play, with scene-setting, characters, and stage directions. The setting is the Pearson International Airport in Toronto, Canada, and at the center of the drama is a Customs officer. These elements are quick clues into a theme and subject that seem to preoccupy the poets in this season of box sets. Again and again, the "border," the place of crossing, the discourses of departure and arrival, of flight, of loss, and the many meanings of home, seem to haunt poet after poet. Some engage the subject directly, while others only suggest, creating a context for the poems, whether they are written by poets fully located in Africa or by those who find themselves crossing back and forth between Africa and elsewhere, or between their home countries and other countries, whether in Africa or outside. Jamila Osman engages the language of migration and nationhood in her title (*A Girl Is a Sovereign State*), and much of the time she employs it as a source of metaphor for understanding the dynamics of gender, the politics of the body, and the practice of selfhood. In "Winter," she shows that all of this must be framed by an understanding of the politics of place, and the border is the grand symbol. And as with so many of the poems in these chapbooks, any exploration of place, migration, or home, is a discussion negotiated through family:

Scene 1:

Location: Toronto Pearson International Airport.
Outside snow softens the unfamiliar landscape, whittles the
    winter's sharp edge.
The Canadian flag flaps in the wind.

Characters: A scowling Customs official in full uniform. A wed-
    ding ring cutting into his finger.
A young woman with no bags, a slip of paper with a phone num-
    ber in her sweaty palm.

Customs official: *Name?*
My girl-mother: *Refugee.*

    It is a violent encounter not because anyone physically assaults the mother but because the language she uses—the words she speaks—is alien to her, and the cold is an assault on her body as it splits open her knuckles and lips.

And in "Girls, Girls, Girls," an elegy to innocence, a poem that addresses her awakening to the troubles in the world, makes clear that the true realities that will overthrow the innocence of girlhood are going to be about the violence with which the alien must contend. And so language is learned to manage the hardship of migration, and at the same time, and most beautifully, Osman connects this theme with her mother.

> Before we learned enough Arabic to perform the funeral prayer,
> Before the first body we mourned was our own.
>
> Before we came to know the geography of our mothers' grief,
> Before we contorted our bodies to fill the shape of her lost country.

For Osman the solution to the vicissitudes of immigration is found inside, it is found in the woman's ability to claim her own sovereignty, having been disappointed by other ways of defining identity: "The body of a girl / is a nation" she says, "with no flag / of its own." At the end of this title poem, she writes, "A girl is a sovereign state. / I will not be a stranger / here / or anywhere." I must admit that when I read a stanza like this, from Safia Jama's *Notes on Resilience,* I grow excited, hungry to read more:

> I was nineteen when my father
> took my picture somewhere near
> the Somali-Ethiopian border.

The reasons should be obvious enough, but they are worth rehearsing. The stanza suggests the value of history and memory—there is a suggestion that an intimacy is being wrestled with and explored. This is the power of the past tense, it is the trust engendered by the first person, and it does reflect the risk. That then, is the draw of time—the way it starts to demand an engagement that is guided by an intimate engagement with history. The second draw is place, and by place, we also mean time and history. So much is contained in the word "border" and even more in the uncertainty and danger of "somewhere near." So much about the geopolitics of Africa, so much about migration, so much about arrivals and departures. What is it that takes bodies to "the Somali-Ethiopian border," and what is being negotiated when a nineteen-year-old woman remembers this instant

in which time is arrested and sealed into memory—a snapshot taken at
a border where two nations are in conflict, at peace, or certainly trying to
work through the divisions of nation, war, and politics. The poem is called
"Two Sisters," and I am reminded of just why this present exploration of
the intimate life of this continent becomes a point of great possibility and
fulfillment for me. The next stanza is as alluring for its detail and its evoca-
tion of the tactile:

> I stood frowning in a flowing dress,
> red fabric loosely covering my hair.

Jama's poem is replete with the themes and ideas that are echoed
throughout this box set. It is simply true that the poets collected here are
negotiating, in the most sophisticated and revealing ways, themes of place,
history, and transition. This may simply be a result of the peculiar intensity
of travel and movement that is the way of the world now. Borders are the
sites of war, of escape, of discovery, of ethnic divisions, and more hopefully,
the sites of imagination remaking, of cross-fertilization, of the strange con-
fluence of cultures and ideas and bodies.

Sadia Hassan has her own borders to traverse—in her case, the Kenya/
Somali border—and she is engaged by the psychic and emotional implica-
tions of border crossings and the meaning of migration.

> In Kenya, I was the woman I had always been: Somali
> refugee, smuggling children yesterday
> and today, a baby goat.
> ["Sujui"]

Indeed, for her there is a comic absurdity to it all, but what I am drawn
to, again and again, is the terrain that she is opening up to us because of the
immediacy of this conversation. Her poem "Smell the Season of Rain Well
Before It Is Upon Us" gifts readers with yet another instant of great promise
and possibility. So much is packed into a few lines:

> In Kenya, my body becomes a tuning
> fork. I arrive in the heat humming, thick
> with surrender.   I heard God loves a

good story and so I returned from the cold
noise of America to repent in earnest for
lonelying my mother, for leaving and
leaving for College.

In poem after poem in this box set, the body figures (as it has in much
poetry from Africa over the last few years) as the subject of rich study
to any enterprising scholar who is interested in discovering intersections
between sexuality, gender, alienation, and self-image and identity in African
writing. Here, the body as "tuning fork" is a splendid metaphor to open the
door to the poems collected here. Migration has a cost, and that cost, bless-
edly, is expressed fruitfully through the tuning bodies of these poets.

For Nkateko Masinga in her chapbook *Psalm for Chrysanthemums*,
while the two destinations of travel she mentions in the book (namely,
South Africa and the US, specifically Richmond, Virginia) are not the
framing of the entire work, we find in her sense of arrival and departure a
metaphor for the more centralized theme, that of emotional and psycho-
logical transport—migration and exile and the quest for home. Here, the
geography of the South African landscape is her source of metaphor, and
so are seasons, so are the names of plants. This is not pastoral verse; instead,
these are poems that show the poet to be alive to a sense of place and the
emotional value of such alertness:

> In my mania, I was the highveld
> with tall plateaus and rolling plains,
> too much hill to fit into this world.
> ["Inpatient"]

And then in America, as a visitor, the alienness is the very pleasure
of her experience of exile. She wants to be away. There is the odd ritual of
fireworks in a country where war is honored and celebrated and in which
war veterans struggle with PTSD. But rather than being traumatized by the
fireworks of the fourth of July, she finds a comfort in the alienness of these
rituals:

> My host mother asked if the fireworks would trigger me,
> if there were wars back home that sounded just like this

and I said, 'I came here to forget what home sounds like.'
["My Lover Pulls Me Off the Train Tracks"]

For Ghanian poet Tryphena Yeboah, the long discourse of her sequence of poems, tantalizingly titled *A Mouthful of Home,* is faith, belief, and religion, and the site for the contestation of this is the intimate relationship between mother, father, and daughter—a conversation of presence, absence, loss, and the discovery of new ways to understand the self as separate from the familial. It is all grounded in Ghana, in its geography, and yet these ideas of migration emerge. Yeboah, too, provides us with these gems about movement, which, though grounded in place, is hardly static, hardly locked to a singular moment.

I TELL MY MOTHER I WANT A BODY THAT EXPANDS
Into a map. She wants to know where I'll travel to. I say "myself."

For her, the journey to self is one that echoes the agenda of all poetry, it seems, but in her exploration of her mother, who figures significantly in these poems, the intimacy is refreshing for its generosity. And by this, I mean that in this openness to sharing her life, Yeboah is generous. In her poem "Honoring What My Family Will Never Know," she writes beautifully:

> Leaving opens us up,
> makes a keeper out of us,
> shows us we're made of more rooms
> than we can count.

This could easily be an epigraph for this collection, and it offers a striking line of examination for so much of what we are seeing in the poetry by the younger generation of African poets. What it reveals is that leaving never quite happens. In fact, leaving is a return, a return to the meaning of the self.

The Adinkra symbol of Akan civilization translates to "farewell," and, given its long association with funeral rituals, one need not think too hard to recognize that movement and transport of the body and the mind serve an elemental role in society. Afua Ansong's poems in her collection, *Try*

Kissing God, allow her to have a conversation with the spirit world, one rooted in Ghanaian philosophy and spiritual beliefs even as they achieve a modernity about arrivals and departures that echoes the rest of these chapbooks.

In her poems, despite their being based in the Ghanaian cultural milieu, one has the sense of departure, as if the poems are all rehearsing the Sankofa symbol of departure and return. This opens the way for a wonderful dance between arrivals and departures, which, in the end, become defining markers of the meaning of "home."

> *if you want to be free you could stop picking,*
> *if you want to run, you can bury yourself,*
> *lie in the field of flowers, white and soft, your burial,*
> *until water pours out of your holes.*
>
> Mother, do not fear.
> The earth itself will drink our blood.
> ["ASASE YƐ DURU"]

Ansong's two-worldness is endemic. It is not, in the Walcottian sense, an even divide, but it is a world in which "home" is interrupted and set in relief by "away." She calls her double-sightedness access to "the best of two worlds." Home, though, is found in her defiant hair—the Africanness of her hair.

> Blessed are those who bantu knot and oil massage their scalps to
>   sleep
> and rise with coconut oil stains on their pillows.
> Blessed are the naturals that plead with dandruffs after a co-wash.
> Blessed are you who transition and possess the best of two
>   worlds.
> Blessed are those who cut and cut until they turn into their roots.
> ["DUAFE"]

And like hair, love is found in this awareness of difference in the poem "ODO NNYEW FIE KWAN" (which translates to "Love never loses its way home"). The lover is likely clandestine—he has a "girlfriend" who is not the speaker, and he is white. But even when he is with her, sharing a bed, he is able to sense her presence and absence. The idea is that love will find home, but the counter idea is that what is happening in the moment is not the "home" that dominates. That is the most haunting:

> You whisper *home is a song to the womb*
> into the green night, your slender fingers
> arched around his wanting ears.
> He tames your clay hands,
> lowers your fingers into his and replies
> *still you must return to it.*

Fatima Camara's familial conversation with the past, with history and with the present in her collection, *Yellow*Line, is inextricably entwined with ideas of departure and arrival, or what she calls "landings." Underneath these discoveries of self, of personal histories and of the repetition of identity, is the looming idea of migration. It is elemental to the throughline of the work:

> I don't remember the first time I met my
> grandmother. I remember before the second
> time thinking there's no way this woman exists.
> We must think we know where to find her.
> This woman who's lost so much must be lost too.
> ["Prep"]

Implicit in this "forgotten" meeting is the narrative of the speaker moving from the myth of a grandmother—one told to her by her mother and others—to meeting her. It is a striking meeting—one characterized by the fulsome and beautiful presence of the grandmother, who never, in these poems, is easily seen as a comfortable part of the speaker. There is a divide, one that Camara is constantly seeking to bridge with poetry, with language. And guiding this process of retrieval is the sea as a symbol of separation and movement.

If you wanted to find the ones that have floated to shore,

the survivors, all around there are plenty of other bodies
that shine like mine.
["Sanno"]

The image is hauntingly familiar—it evokes the bodies of refugees
strewn on the beaches of Europe after the Mediterranean crossing. This is
now a constant trope in much of the poetry and fiction of Africa. It is not
an invention nor a fancy. Yet for Camara, there is another body of water,
one she calls "the mid-Atlantic ridge," where she imagines her grandmother
has died, where she has become "a seabed." Yet this death is a moment of
reclamation and restoration:

> My grandmother
> is no longer
> one who has met her end
> but who has gone back to the beginning.
>
> Till she is the seabed.
> Till she is the land kicked back
> to the surface.
> ["Erosion"]

In her poem "Repetition," however, Camara lays out the deep-seated
anxieties and complexities of familial divides caused by migration or the
prospect of migration. These are not poems of geopolitical polemics, but
these are poems that go further, that help us to see the consequences of
migration:

> She taught, I learned. We understand different.
>
> Two different countries, we move different.
> From where did you come, child? she asks.
>
> Always the questions that aren't really asked.
> From a woman whose body rejects this land.
>
> I scream that I didn't choose this landing.

She screams that this land did not make me.

So I wait for her to recognize me.
We wake and in front of a mirror, we stand.

It is hopeful, this ending, this way in which the speaker recognizes
herself in her mother's body, a body that is acutely alienated in a new land, a
new "landing." These poems are a reclamation of an African self, one that is
shaped and reimagined through language.

Hennh Kyereh Kwaku, of all the poets in this set, is most explicitly
engaged with the wider world. His sardonic wit and cutting critique of
postcolonial society constantly position the meaning of Ghana against
what Ghana is not—the forces that are collapsing on Ghana and forcing
the country to react. He is interested in the relationship between the cedi
and the franc and the dollar. He is fully aware of the dangerous presence of
the Chinese in West Africa and the compromises that are leading to this
circumstance—the corruption and the desperation. While Kwaku is not ex-
plicitly engaged by migration as a trope of self and identity, his awareness of
Ghanaian modernity within the wider world in his collection "Revolution
of Scavengers," and its construction of a genuine global economy, puts into
stark relief the meaning of nation, the meaning of self, and the meaning of
cultural identity.

> I still don't understand why Ghana & Nigeria do not
> add up. *Sweat too na water abi?* Let the Chinese come
> for the bauxite at Atiwa & show us how to fetch sweat
> for distillation. *Na only sweat we dey get from the sun
> o, but we shun the solar energy. Or sweat be wonna solar
> energy?* Ra, we know—the God of the sun.
> ["Even in Our Differences There's a Similarity"]

Kwaku, writing from the heart of the fulcrum, is fully aware of the ways
in which the very notion of country, of flag, of sovereignty is constantly
being contested by the circumstances of history. His postcolonial discourse
is refreshing in the way it shakes up certain overused tropes that either seek
to dismiss the persistence of colonialism and imperialism, or that remain

fixated on those two forces as the sole arbiters of African destruction. Instead, Kwaku reminds us that nothing is that simple. A new discourse, for example, has to operate around the Chinese. In the poem "In This Mine We Pray," he asks, "Is it xenophobic to protect my water from Chinese miners?" These are tough questions, and poetry allows him to venture there:

> Do not take yourself from the action & say: *they took GHC 1.00 from me.* Say: *I bribed the police.* Blame yourself. Do not say our flag does not dance when between the French & the American flag—our flag is cotton & shy, not just anything blows it away—so was this country made. This is your country. Our flag is not on any missile meant to wipe half of the world—our presidents are not Thanos to snap & wipe. We'd rather snap & get Noah's Ark for Accra before the floods.
> ["Anything for the Boys?"]

In poem after poem, what grows increasingly clear in Kwaku's work is that much of what is to be understood about Ghana, about Accra and its vulnerability to floods and drought, is as much defined by what happens in the country as it is by what happens outside. In a revealing and deeply honest anecdote in the poem "Welcoming a Ghanaian God," Kwaku offers an indirect but critical commentary on migration and the ways in which the definition of migrant is as important to those who have been left behind as it is to those who have left:

> About a month ago, Kofi Kingston became WWE's first African-born world champion, his mother says he's a full Ghanaian. Not African-American. Not Ghanaian-American—he's not hyphenated. He's full. She makes me believe again that being Ghanaian is something to be proud of.

Egyptian poet Nadra Mabrouk is a woman in transition between cultures in her chapbook *Measurements of Holy*. But like so many of the poets in this set, the most vital stage for the enactment of the drama of migration is the relationship between the mother and the daughter.

My mother on the phone
is upset that I still remember her sitting
on the kitchen floor of her mother's
apartment in Shobra, plucking feathers
from the mottled bodies of geese, their insides
jeweled and engorged on their own shimmering,
their necks hanging over her wrists
like unclasped bracelets.
["Autumn, Spiraling"]

Her mother is the connection to memory and to Cairo. It is a connection to childhood, and it is a troubled and uncertain memory because it is associated with the divide between home and what is not home, or what has become another home. Importantly, what the poet remembers, the image of her mother plucking goose feathers, is an image that upsets her mother. Mabrouk does not explain why. She merely leaves this negotiating between memory and the present as a point of rupture and uncertainty.

Thus in her poem "Portrait of the Country in Which I Was Born," that country is a child and at the same time a body, not unlike the lost mother who resists memory, resists being reduced to a memory by being an unruly memory. In a striking image, Mabrouk locates one of the core dilemmas of migration—the fact that the "home place," or the place of contested origin, is not a static place, even if it feels that way in memory. The poet is frustrated by the subject who simply won't keep still:

We can barely hear anything now over this display,

desperate for memory, I need you to hold still so that we may get
    this right.
Here is a knife, I will be quicker this time. I will even sing you a song.

The collection is soaked in a haunting sense of loss, not merely within the poet herself, but also in those around her, and especially in the parents. It may seem obvious enough to point this out, but it is worth reflecting on the extent to which so many of these poets recognize the dilemmas of movement—even in the prospect of otherness, of simply looking outside of home from home, for the security and stability of "home" which is being threatened and tested. In the beautiful portrait of her father as a young man in Egypt, Mabrouk imagines the father's departure before it happens:

> how your mother was crying
> of a dream in which the hand
> of every person you ever loved
> was reaching for you from a river
> whose current surged, their fingers swelling
> in the progress, palms barely recognizable,
> African tigerfish swarming again and again.
> ["Father as Adolescent, Smoking"]

Adedayo Adeyemi Agarau in *The Origin of Name* offers us a sense of what happens when a poet insists on the quest for a grounding in "home," in tradition and in the rituals of an ancient culture in the face of modernity. Indeed, as if in response to the turmoil and upheaval of travel, movement, and alienation from home, Agarau presents a meditation on the importance of having a grounding in the spiritual practices of the society as a preparation to travel, to venture outside of home. It is this grounding that allows movement to be possible.

> The gods ask us to bring salt and sprinkle it on this soil,
> to beckon earth mothers to rise from flames,
> to give us dreams wide enough to ferry us,
> to build us a boat and name each land a city across the sea,
> give us feathers and wings and letters and names.
> ["The Gods Ask Us to Make an Oasis"]

In his poem "Bantale Drowning in the Flower Room," Agarau is clearly thinking of those who are exiled aliens living in society and those from "home" who have left and are living in exile. Without commenting on the ethical or even political implications of exile, he observes narratives of travel, of exile—narratives that we have seen have captured the imagination of so many of the poets included here; rather than merely speaking to the hardships of travel, of migration and movement, they offer a reminder of the value of "home." It is this seeming contradiction that permeates the work we encounter here:

> Perhaps each of your exiles
> is a reminder that home
> is the paradise of woods.

Michelle K. Angwenyi's poems are careful internal quarrels—the world outside of the mind, the working through of the self that is muted except when she is constructing a sense of place as a way to understand feeling and thought. The title of her collection, *Gray Latitudes,* invokes ideas of geography and place. But in the poems, she is employing these ideas in largely metaphorical ways—the latitudes represent the lines that separate what is understood and what she is wrestling to understand. Yet in her first poem, "Memorial," the language of travel, of arrivals and departures, is employed in ways that align with the work of other poets in the series:

> These are the elaborate one-sided goodbyes.
> The learning to accept tea from strangers.
> The voiceless convergence of winds.
>
> —
>
> . . .
>
> The slowness of arrival. The always arriving.
> The day, and its salt pillars.
> And the sun, still water.

In the one poem that names her home city and offers a striking and evocative portrait of the city, Angwenyi reminds us that often "home" is understood best in juxtaposition to what it is not.

> In this place of colliding times,
> no word for it in childhood, and unrecognizable in this dusk,
> Nairobi comes and goes.
> I had the word for it yesterday,

and the need that follows, to remember that feeling:
too-long trousers, newspaper kites, lost boys
and now, grown-up absences via the labyrinths of other cities.
["Part II: Gray Latitudes"]

Nairobi, described as a place of "colliding times," is indeed a city with a relative history of hosting many interlopers and of various cultures imposing on Kikuyu and Massai land. During the nineteenth century, the city was at the heart of all the great changes in that country—all the collisions of people and movements. Yet the Nairobi she speaks of here is illusive and changeable, which is part of its beauty. In the end, its meaning is found in the "absences," the movement of people from Nairobi to "other cities." It is in this sense that Angwenyi reflects what Patricia Jabbeh Wesley says in her introduction to the chapbook. She sees in Angwenyi, and by extension in the new generation of African poets, a refreshing new possibility:

> Gray Latitudes defies all norms by navigating the
> modern literary landscape of the African at home and
> abroad—a new domain that invites us all to write our
> Africa in its complete modernity and tradition, whatever
> that is in the new world.

—*Kwame Dawes*

PART TWO
The Horse of Language

When you are engaged primarily in facilitating the production of a yearly curated list of books, you are engaged with the frenetic energy that comes with it—deadlines, negotiation, fundraising, and the never-ending process of selecting, editing, and juxtaposing books like tracks on an old-school EP. In the matrix of that kind of energy, it is hard to contend with big-picture matters like trends, canons, or even the journey so far. For that, editors have to rely on critical readers, scholars, and other poets.

Appropriately, Kwame has chosen the Akan word *Sankofa* as the title for his section of the introduction. A deeply West African word, Sankofa is simultaneously a word, a proverb, a symbol, an Adrinka ideograph that implies (please note that I have chosen not to say "means;" I chose the word implies because almost every word in any West African language—and this includes names—is an elision of complex ideas and stories so that we can only imply the possibilities it is addressing) a kind of looking back in order to move forward. A sort of curatorial review.

And in keeping with the spirit of Sankofa, the insights he gleans serve only as general signposts on an ongoing journey but never claim any singular authority on knowing. Always it is about a gleaning, an implying. In a way these introductions have come to be simultaneous conversations between Kwame and me, the editors and the readers, the whole list of the African Poetry Book Fund and a kind of Western Canon, the editors and the poets (not only those we have published but those we are yet to publish). They are conversations with the wider world of African scholarship, with the tradition, and with an African artistic and philosophical worldview. Communicating the complexity of these negotiations in just a few words requires us to write clearly, definitively even, but open-ended.

Proverbs, the distillation of a complex wisdom to an image, is as complex in human thought as a quantum entanglement. In Yoruba, a proverb, Owe, is called the horse language rides. In other words, the implication is that language is not a fixed system of meaning as we are often taught to think of it in Western (or should I say modern capitalist?) thought. As we say in my small town of origin, Afikpo, language is a river that flows toward the future carrying the knowledge of before into the possibility of now. One can think of a poem, a prayer, a song, or even just an exclaimed sound as a proverb—the horse that all the ineffable hopes of our human self rides in language, a gesture always fluttering in time and space. Poetry has as its central concern language itself. Language and its slippery forms. It feels sometimes that in all African languages there is more fluidity in the articulations of self than in the languages that are more deeply mired in the transactions of capital. I am not pointing to any primitivism here in thought or scholarship (because these languages are more complex than current Western forms) but only stating that precisely because these languages haven't been at the heart of global capitalism, they haven't been reduced to a mere transactional state. They hold simultaneity and occasional convergence with ease, having no need to fall into either side of one single transaction.

African thought, particularly West African thought (and the expression of such in dense forms is the proverb), visualizes life and all its attendants as the concept of journey, of travel. So many proverbs are expressions of travel in time, space, and conceptualization. Here are a few to think about: to get lost is to learn the way; by crawling a child learns to stand; by trying often the monkey learns to jump from the tree; nobody is born wise; you learn to cut down trees by cutting them down; you don't teach the paths of the forest to an old gorilla; traveling is learning. I could go on ad infinitum. We see the ideas of presence as a doubling back, but also as a moving forward in time, space, width, length, and breadth and interiority. These are at the heart of our linguistic DNA as Africans, and therefore the composition of our worldview, which is that of convergence and multiplicity. In other words, time (and therefore all measurable phenomena) becomes, as the Yoruba say, La-Lai, or, as the Igbo say, Akile—an entanglement. At once converging into a "moment" before fracturing into simultaneity. Even the rituals of Africa are designed as a journey—even the construction of prayers and proverbs—and so it follows that poems are made from this deeply embedded matrix, and they must therefore carry these dimensionalities inside them.

So, then, we ask what does any of that have to do with this chapbook box set? Well, everything and maybe nothing. Perhaps you will have to be the judge of that. But here is the thing, the bulk of the work we are reading is grouped around the idea of identity. Surely everything is, you might say. But in this case the identity explored is different and specific. There was a time within African life and thought that identity involved distancing ourselves from the colonial oppression that had lasted on the continent for, in some cases, well over a hundred years and also indirectly, for another three hundred before that, by way of destructive commerce with the Portuguese and the British, and also of course with the trade in humans as slaves.

The identity that was forged through postcolonialism was national rather than more humanist or even modernist. Such identities became essentialized very quickly. So much of what we think of as identity was assumed and conflated with nation and forged in response to Western incursion. We seldom came to these modern—or perhaps a better word is recent—selves in the modern literatures post-independence via a slow accretion of a modernist arc. We instead assumed common constructed selves (so constructed in response to whiteness and heterosexual patriarchy; after all, the nation was the all Father) and wrote in "epic" voices that addressed in bombast. We were mainly praise singers chanting big songs in support of a shaky, often unquestioned, essential identity. In very much the same way that masculinity is forged in a series of evacuated negatives (as in, I am a man because I am not . . . and we return to this and fathers later), this new identity, and even the poetics of its address, was constructed in the same way. The flow and flex of a poetics in flux, journey and uncertainty of language and the mediation of self via the multiplicities articulated above, gave way to this new misconstrued "modern" approach. Almost a propaganda of what we were and were not. The journey at the heart of identity via language as ritual, as the vehicle of the ineffable, was suppressed. In that context, the novel, already seen as the vehicle of identity and nation in the West, took leadership. Poetry, and the gift of slippage and question, got lost in the mix or took the form of verse masking the heart of prose. We see this still to a large extent in contemporary American poetry.

As Kwame points out, immigration is considered the pressing issue of the twenty-first century, and he gestures toward Toni Morrison's beautiful take on it in her book *The Origin of Others* (and we are aware that there are many other examples that could have been cited). And while it is true that migration/immigration—forced (and much of it is about displacement, loss, and poverty) and voluntary (better deployment of skills and abilities, etc.)—is at the cutting edge of the century, it's not true that it is new or a sudden phenomenon (not that Kwame is arguing that it is). We are all familiar with the fear and expression of the barbarians at the gate. The unique challenges of this century are scale (the sheer numbers are overwhelming), the privilege of host populations that place immigrant populations at a disadvantage educationally and with fewer skill sets, the neglected pressures of climate change and the impact on resources, the unchecked capitalism and the ever-growing gulf between those who have and don't have, and many more such pressures mean that the patterns of movement and the direction of flow is overwhelmingly one-directional. So then, in the new flex, we finally have to contend with assertions like those by Homi Bhabha that "identity is not a destination, it's a state of flux," as visceral realities and not just mental and academic jumps in conceptual territories while bodies remain static (sometimes with the fixed essential identities mentioned before). Whatever else the anxieties might be, this provides real and exciting opportunities for discovery within African literature. With novels still locked so heavily in place defending long-since-defunct territories (this does not of course include exciting forms like speculative fiction and sci-fi, to name just two), poetry can, with its innate ability to shape narratives while not being married to the sequential flow of time and space, step up to ask and explore the resulting questions.

In these new poetic forms and voices, we find that the essential identities of the past fall easily away, and the loss that we are left with gives rise to the need for more individual and nuanced explorations resulting in the proliferation of negotiations that Kwame so elegantly and effortlessly lays bare in his section, relying entirely on the work as an evidentiary offering—and what a rich one it is. This quest here is a form of modernism, but a form that is not what we are used to thinking of, which is a modernist approach in relation to Western philosophy, which positions itself as the next real jump after that so wrongly named age of enlightenment. This, what we encounter here, is a return to that much more complex and advanced philosophy of self that the African past offers. Our languages of expression and the ideas behind them, even via the colonial oppressions of English, French, Spanish, and Portuguese remain in flux, fluid and flexible, waiting for new horsemen and horsewomen to ride it into the twenty-first century. Hold that thought.

That many of these poets reside in the diaspora is not a limitation but a necessity because the truth is that the continent of Africa is a complex negotiation of internal diasporas. Hausas range from Senegal through Nigeria and into Cameroon. Yorubas from Western Nigeria through to Sierra Leone, and the same for Igbos. In fact some scholars argue that the idea of a Yoruba nation results in smaller nations expanding into empires and occupying territories that held other nations. And they go further to argue that the word Yoruba is from the ethnic nation of Nupe, bordering the old Oyo empire, and is a Nupe word that means "those people." So, where else to make sense of a fractured identity than in cultures, and places where there is so much pressure on essentialism that questions that could not be asked at home must be confronted abroad? Remember the Yoruba and Lai-Lai? It's all an entanglement, and the very least of it is that we come back to the original horse of language, the home of self. Hold that thought.

For a long time, Kwame and I were trying to encourage a very particular African poetics to develop. We have tried to allow this evolution to happen as organically as we can. We have nudged scholars, poets, and even reviewers to consider this angle, but of all the demographics, it is the poets themselves who have generated the general outlines of a distinctly African Poetics through the variety and strength of the work itself. So in this chapbook box set, the eighth in the series, and nearly 100 chapbooks in, we are finally seeing not so much a trend or trends but a deep struggle to figure out what African literary Modernism can be. We are seeing the true articulation of identity from multiple points of view, rather than an embrace or push away from an essential monolithic identity—a conversation generated, sustained, and trusted outside of simple binaries and whose textual referents are generated in the process and not from already existing ideological positions. A way forward, a new horse of language.

—*Chris Abani*

KWAME DAWES is the author of twenty-one books of poetry and numerous other books of fiction, criticism, and essays. In 2016, his book *Speak from Here to There*, a cowritten collection of verse with Australian poet John Kinsella, was released along with *When the Rewards Can Be So Great: Essays on Writing and the Writing Life,* which Dawes edited. His most recent collection, *City of Bones: A Testament,* was published in 2017. His awards include the Forward Poetry Prize, the Hollis Summers Poetry Prize, the Musgrave Silver Medal, several Pushcart Prizes, the Barnes & Nobles Writers for Writers Award, and an Emmy Award. He is the Glenna Luschei Editor of *Prairie Schooner* and is Chancellor Professor of English at the University of Nebraska. Dawes serves as the associate poetry editor for Peepal Tree Press and is director of the African Poetry Book Fund. He is the artistic director of the Calabash International Literary Festival. In 2018, he was elected a chancellor of the Academy of American Poets.

Claus gretter

CHRIS ABANI's prose includes *The Secret History of Las Vegas*, *Song for Night*, *The Virgin of Flames*, *Becoming Abigail*, *GraceLand*, and *Masters of the Board*. His poetry collections are *Sanctificum*, *There Are No Names for Red*, *Feed Me the Sun*, *Hands Washing Water*, *Dog Woman*, *Daphne's Lot*, and *Kalakuta Republic*. He holds a BA in English, an MA in gender and culture, an MA in English, and a PhD in literature and creative writing. Abani is the recipient of a PEN USA Freedom to Write Award, a Prince Claus Award, a Lannan Literary Fellowship, a California Book Award, a Hurston/Wright Legacy Award, a PEN Beyond Margins Award, a PEN/Hemingway Award, and a Guggenheim Award. Born in Nigeria, he is currently Board of Trustees Professor of English at Northwestern University in Chicago.

Tariku Shiferaw is a New York–based artist who explores "mark-making" through painting and installation art in order to address the physical and metaphysical spaces of painting and societal structures. He was raised in Los Angeles and currently lives and works in New York. Shiferaw's current exhibitions include *Men of Change,* with the Smithsonian Institution Traveling Exhibition, and *Unbound* at the Zuckerman Museum of Art. In Fall 2019, Shiferaw exhibited in a group show titled *What's Love Got to Do With It?* at the Drawing Center in New York. Other exhibitions include the 2017 Whitney Biennial, as part of Occupy Museum's *Debtfair* project; *A Poet*hical Wager* at the Museum of Contemporary Art Cleveland; a 2017 solo exhibition titled *Erase Me* at Addis Fine Art in London; and a 2018 solo show titled *This Ain't Safe* at Cathouse Proper in Brooklyn. From 2018 through 2020, he participated in the Independent Study Studio Program at the Whitney Museum of American Art; Open Sessions at the Drawing Center; and the LES Studio Program in New York City. In March 2020, he began a new artist residency at the World Trade Center through the organization Silver Art Projects. Shiferaw's work has been published in the *New York Times,* the *Washington Post, Hyperallergic,* and *Art In America,* among many other publications.

ENUMERATION
SADIA HASSAN

Published by Akashic Books
©2020 Sadia Hassan

ISBN: 978-1-61775-879-9

Akashic Books
Brooklyn, New York, USA
Twitter: @AkashicBooks
Facebook: AkashicBooks
E-mail: info@akashicbooks.com
Website: www.akashicbooks.com

African Poetry Book Fund
Prairie Schooner
University of Nebraska
110 Andrews Hall
Lincoln, Nebraska 68588

TABLE OF CONTENTS

PREFACE
by Matthew Shenoda

In Sadia Hassan's *Enumeration*, we are introduced to a visceral and skillful poet concerned with the ways black life is understood across geographies. Hassan's language develops into a tender and nuanced look at the intersections of location and lives, layered by movements both political and physical. Like the enumeration alluded to in her title poem, the poems collected here keep count of the litanies of memory, the tolls taken on the bodies of women, and the border crossings that come one after another until finally somewhere can be called "home." In "I Smell the Season of Rain Well Before It Is Upon Us," she upends the idea of home being fixed and, instead, opts for a sense of knowing the intimate feel of a place, fleeting or not:

> Garissa is not home, but it is familiar
> the way a burn is familiar. It cools after months of blistering
> heat.

It is within this sense of familiarity that much of Hassan's poetry takes shape. As shown in the title poem, "Enumeration," she is interested not just in the telling of a history or the chronicling of lives, but in the ways in which these lives and histories are shaped by the various affinities that intersect them:

> I keep recounting the hours,
> the light inking the edges
> of the morning
> without permission,
> the prickly sweet smell of the air,
> the street and it's dizzying din.

4

In this way, Hassan's poetry always feels grounded, rooted in a context—there is an awareness deeply familiar to the speaker. It is that sense of grounding that allows her to clearly articulate the political realities that shape her life and that of so many of the African diaspora. When Hassan speaks of the violation of women and the brutality and brutalization of men, whether interpersonally or by the state, she does so having given the reader a clear and unambiguous sense of the bodies being subjugated:

> For months it does not rain,
>   and then, after the breaking—
> after his friend forces his way in to my
> room, on to my bed, between myself and
> myself—it rains. A rain black with flies
> that pools in ruts
> that buckles the gutters
> and muddies the bottom
> of my skirts.

Hers is not a political poetry driven by ideology but one derived from realism that has been formed in the details of the life she has lived and encountered—one that the reader has been made to understand through the deep-seated and unfeigned worldliness of her lines. She writes with a deliberateness that allows us to know what that experience really means; it is tethered not to idea or ideal, but to a person—in the flesh. She goes on in this vein:

> Men think
> they can take what they like
> as if no one will miss it,
> but I have always missed
> what was taken from me
> without permission.

> I wake some mornings bloated
> with missing.

By the time we reach these lines in "Enumeration," we too are in the throes of missing.

Hassan's poems manage to draw attention to the fidelities of the intergenerational and cross-continental dynamics operating in her world, and they do so by embracing the dualities or multimodal senses of self, as in "Sujui."

> I was only a diaspora
> girl, and not a single soul
> expected propriety.

While not adhering to the propriety that might be expected by some, Hassan in these poems has created a decorum of her own. She demonstrates the possibilities that come with a new way of seeing, one that does not settle for well-worn tropes. In doing this, she is emblematic of a new generation of African poets that happily draw on a complex of different traditions that have shaped their sense of self.

SUJUI

The Tana river, red and roiling
swelled with rain the summer after
I left school,

and I kept quiet
what I found there buried
like a sweet in my mouth.

The aunties would say
I'd become a woman
wild with youth.

I was only a diaspora
girl, and not a single soul
expected propriety.

I spent the summer
flushed, finessing men
out of hotel dinners,

perfecting the precise
lift of my shoulders,
meant to coyly answer
the questions:

Wapi Kitambulisho?

Where is my identity?
Sujui.

Being careful
not to mean *I am Somali–*
Kenyan
which is a truth
where I simply meant
to be difficult: *I do not know.*

Once on my way to the camps
to see my small-mom,
I held a goat in my lap too long,
forgetting my inheritance.

The red-hatted soldier with his one hooded eye
declared my passport counterfeit.

In Kenya, I was the woman I had always been: Somali
refugee, smuggling children yesterday
and today, a baby goat.

All at once, the whispers: just last summer
another young girl, the same soldier, her dress,
how, in the mirror, as the bus pulled away,
her eyes fell.

Sujui not being enough,
I said *Mzee, I am an American.*

And I declared myself this way
until he understood I could not be
that other woman, that the goat

was not mine
and neither was Garissa,
this city of dust
and so on and so on.

I SMELL THE SEASON OF RAIN
WELL BEFORE IT IS UPON US

In Kenya, my body becomes a tuning
fork. I arrive in the heat humming, thick
with surrender.   I heard God loves a
good story and so I returned from the cold
noise of America to repent in earnest for
lonelying my mother, for leaving and
leaving for College.

 A man promising to take me to my father's
family says the dust and desert scrub of
Garissa will heal me of my haunting.

In the meantime, My Uncle tells me to relax,
we are home.

                                        I do not relax.

                    Garissa is not home, but it is familiar
                    the way a burn is familiar. It cools after
                    months of blistering heat.   I catch a cold.
                        I cover and cover my mouth, my hands,
                    my ass—and still—the fumble of flashlights
                    slippery as night falling, the cool kiss of
                    limestone on puckered flesh.

Now that I am a whore, I
must practice.

The boy I am necking is eighteen and
familiar. Meaning he loves me without
listening.

At night, I perch on the deck deliciously
washed waiting for the siren of crickets to
overtake the pattering of rain. I wrap my
legs around his waist. Above him this way,
I am exquisite.

                      The body is a premonition.

                    For months it does not rain,
                          and then, after the breaking—
                  after his friend forces his way in to my
                  room, on to my bed, between myself and
                  myself—it rains. A rain black with flies
                  that pools in ruts
                  that buckles the gutters
                  and muddies the bottom
                  of my skirts.

I try to remember.

No man is the first.

He could not possibly have known
at eighteen, at twenty-two, how a city
in August
can conjure the armpit stink of another
in October

                    that a damp whisper
                    is enough
               to alter the gate and gravel
               of our compound
               into the lap I lingered on
                    at eight
               thinking a man's beard
               can feel so much
               like a loosening scream.

I pretend it does not matter			how this ends.

And yet, it does. The city does not pitch me
out. Nothing bursts or breaks. No one turns
to the stand, your honor. No man is
swallowed by the silence or witched to
stone.

Each is allowed peace: to marry
and otherwise walk living and limbed
among us.

The end?				The sky remains blue and clear most days
it is just difficult to breathe.

JESUS AT WYNFIELD STATION

Remember 1997, when we were here a year
in this new country? Every limb an instrument
we could not make sing?

Our small girl bodies felled and risen
from the dead
until we found our feet and ran?

We did not know how to walk
in this new skin blackening suddenly before us

until our brothers, brave and braggadocios, taught us
how to *Nigga* with our mouths leaning; our tongues
sneak full of all the clanging they claimed to be English.

What mama called *no language at all.*
No culture, neither.

Remember mama, and the roaches?
How they overran the house, flew over our heads?

And all seven of us, huddled in the empty of our living room
while she swatted with bare hands at everything—the ceiling,
our feet, her own nervous trembling mouth

until, finally, the white man arrived and she led him
to the bathroom where we watched him jump back
pink with fright.

JESUS!

And they came forth, a sea of black
roaches crawling towards the light.

Yes! Jesus! Mama said,
Jesus fly-fly everywhere!

And everywhere Jesus flew we found ourselves
what we must have looked like at the border
naked and black and trembling, the years
splayed open-legged before us.

INTERLUDE IN MY LOVER'S MOUTH

Twenty-five and unprepared
for the bitterness of grief

I wear my lover like a cross
and in the lush

ditch of my mouth
I ruin him with my need.

He says *shhhhh*
He says *mmmh,*
                  your body

and I hear   *a soft peach*
                wet with teeth

We make with our bodies
our mistakes, twenty-

six and crying out
deliciously as a woman

when she misremembers
running and calls it sleep

In sleep
I sour myself
with the rot of him

I shiver and shiver each breast
into his mouth

and slick with sweat
it seems

hmmm, your body
is dead weight one carries on their tongue
and   (quiet as it's kept)
there is no *where*
to bury it.

He says *shhhhh*
He says *hmmm,*
                    your body

and I hear   *running*

is the beginning
of the story.

ENUMERATION

1.
I am made smaller
in my shame
for remembering

something happened

and I did not
stop it.

In truth I could
not.

In all honesty I did not know
I could not.

2.
I keep recounting the hours,
the light inking the edges
of the morning
without permission,
the prickly sweet smell of the air,
the street and its dizzying din.

For years, I kept prayer
over the evenings spent laughing with my father

as if they may never again
happen
as easily
as the notebook, the camera, the wallet
disappeared.

3.
I wake up one day in a city
I've lonelied with my leaving
noting the newness of my life.

I cannot tell you how,
or I can.

I did not die
from the shame,
that's how.

I memorized
my responsibilities,
paid my bills.

But it is hard when I begin my long walk
to the farmer's market
in the middle of the afternoon
on a day I leave home in a hurry
and suddenly
a fact I had hoped to forget:

a woman's body
can be cleaved
fresh as torn earth
and no one
not even her mother
can put it back right.

Did you know?

4.
Men think
they can take what they like
as if no one will miss it,
but I have always missed
what was taken from me
without permission.

I wake some mornings bloated
with missing.

I root for it in the cupboard,
the missing; and I root for it
in the dirt.

My hair, the men, their hands,
the missed and the missing
being all that remains
for lifetimes after, decaying
the years, brutalizing the hours.

A CATALOG OF FEARS

*

These days my parents pursue a new ritual: gathering nightly the pulse of tragedy
  in as many countries as they have family.   Somalia, Australia, Britain, Kenya, Syria, Iraq,
Libya, Egypt, Eritrea, Ethiopia, Mexico.   I once arrived from the airport to my parents
watching what I thought was a home video: thirty-one people killed, forty wounded
  in a restaurant bombing.   Civilians picking up rubble.   The soundtrack? A song
my father once sang to my mother while she washed the dishes.

*

                It worries me.
All they love is a drone strike   from becoming a memorial I think about
    as my mother is building a house on the coast of Kismayo.   I look up
at the redwoods from an opposite coast,   in my hand a WhatsApp video of my mother
    on a rickety boat crossing the Jubba.   I think that red is either as deep
  as the blood coming out in the wash   or as dark as the clay in Southern Utah.   My sister
  who says the Rez is just a refugee camp with liquor stores sends me a photo of my nephew
awkwardly scuffing his Jays on the deck of a sailboat. Abdul is surrounded by whites
at his new private school.   He looks unhappy.   I want to send the photo to my mother
but realize they've never spoken.

*

In Minneapolis, Philando Castile's murderer is quietly acquitted of all charges and his mother
says   *I don't give a fuck what you do. Do what your heart desires!*   I cry.
No justice, no peace. Philando, dead a day before my brother's birthday who I wanted to call
but couldn't on account of I was out on the freeway where I had no business,   is silent.

*

The night is loud
  the way a cookout is loud.
    The air, tight and still
as the moment before an earthquake.   A man plays his trumpet so smooth
                          it drowns out the sirens, the bleating,
                          the roaring below on the streets.

  No Justice. No Peace. No Justice. No Peace.

    I imagine a chorus. Angels
    keeping salat at the edge
    of his grave, I imagine
    him keening.

          I   shouldn't

be here. It seems
no one knows where I should be.

                    *

          It's true.

I have run out of things to run from,   my shame included. No one
                          ends up on a bridge

23

where they have no business   and I would have told them as much.   That I keep
   calling my brother brother hoping he'll cry on the phone.   That I keep looking around
wanting to belong   to a city
              that itself
   does not belong.   That a year from now I would be staring at Khadija Saye's tinotypes
   wondering
   who
                    had any business in that building?

                                   *

                  No one
     asks
     what it is like
to wake up
to your parents
keeping watch
over the world's unlanguageable silence.

It is a kind of homecoming.

              We sit nightly through years of YouTube footage,
              mirroring their rapt attention.

              Once it was a wedding. Once a concert
              and the performer played all the way through.

              Once, at a club and they could not hear
              his dying over the music.

*

Obama gives his last speech and my parents
gather their American Children in their sitting room
to translate.

> I make thermos after thermos of tea, watching my father
> miss his mouth as my mother sings.

> > All the niggas we love are a bullet
> > away

from disappearing,   and all our parents, collecting money
for the janazza on WhatsApp.

A BOY WAS KILLED IN CLARKSTON

AFTER GWENDOLYN BROOKS

And I heard it up the block
in Oakland.
His face the same face I held
to the couch,
he and my brother
having stolen ice cream money
from the cushion for calling cards.

All the internet will tell me, I already
know. Yes, his parents fled a coup
same as mine, fled the war;
and he played
for the Fugees; and he cried
during Oprah; and cried
during leg lifts and sit ups
and especially
when they called him fatboy.

What they won't tell me is
that he died at all.

That a boy was killed
in Clarkston that I had walked
to school once.

That a boy died. A boy
from Clarkston.

And now my own parents are nursing the news

of a gun.

I keep
asking the internet
but did he die though? Is he dead?

And I keep asking the internet
how? Or, at least,
can you tell me what to do
with all the unknowing
years between us
suckling this dry bone?

My therapist says
there is only the *now*
but there is also the now
of when my mother last saw him
in the plaza, all six feet of him
doubling over for a hug.

She said she felt
his familiar weight,
his face fat in her hands,
smile sweet as cream.

And the men, shamed
at the tenderness
between them,
walked back into their shops
at the sight.

A CATALOG OF PRAISE

Praise the coffeeshop one block up from the crib
and praise the black barista in purple with a newborn
and up at seven making white folks coffee.
Praise her sister's bald head shining and liner
cut crisper than a mug
and praise the laugh skipping like a record
and the mug chipped
from the weak shelf of the start-up
that stole my two good years and praise
the two good years however they found me
sweet or unsweet.
And praise my daddy for calling me sweetness
and praise my daddy for pilfering sugar
and praise my daddy for refusing silence and praise my daddy
for edging my mother towards a gentle hello and good
on her for trusting I would return to the table and rise
from the bed—praise the bed, and these days, the table
set with tea and the one succulent I almost killed
leaning long-tongued towards me and not the sun.
And praise the viridescent and decaying
heavy. Praise the air between these lungs
and the funk between these pits.
Praise my name, Ya Allah,
praise my lips, hips, and eye sockets
for beholding another day.
Praise the days for keeping on coming.
Praise the good earth and the night terrors
and the wonders of a small cup of coffee and one
chocolate croissant.

MY FATHER WATCHES MICHELLE OBAMA GARDEN
WHILE MAMA COOKS

And it is strange, no?

What a woman does with her hands
when no one is looking?

And stranger still, the way a man will watch her mouth
stung with hunger as she extolls the delight of sweet potatoes,
wanting to know if they taste *good*.

My father is so sweet he says everything
must taste *good* on the lips of a woman
with that much money, but we know money
don't make a woman *good*
or full or happy just as dirt don't clean

a woman's hands if there's blood
in the water or a man willing to slaughter
a she-goat, blank an entire village
of Palestinians, smoke the back
of a wedding from the sky
while she gardens.

and look, look—this is my father
talking, a simple man
who oversaw a sugar mill in Somalia
and not a country in occupied territory—
but can you imagine?

What *good* my own mama's hands
had been careful not to burn down
as my father, simple as a life sentence,
turned from the sight of gristle
on the grill?

WHAT THE LIVING DO

FOR JAMILA AND AYAN OSMAN

Across from me, the yellow hat she wore just outside
on the porch where we smiled at the boys walking past
with all of our teeth showing.

And the black sweater I stole last week; her bag, also black
and the candy inside it, melting. All month we've moved
from one light-filled room to the next, fingers sticky
with sugar or stinking of smoke.

In Phoenix, on the side of the road she wept and I
sat cool and still, ready for the comfort of a mess
we could fix with both of our hands.

It was the song
on the radio and the road between us,
the Grand Canyon staticky with a year
that began with a bone in her throat.

I think of her sister and my own, all the sisters
we've lost together and alone.

I want to tell her
my mom once left a country and returned in the heat of summer
to smell the earth she buried my sister in while I slept
in a forest in Mendocino County, wet with a rain that promised

nothing: no death of baby sisters, no car crashes, no love songs
no one will dance to at weddings we cannot attend because
once dead, there is no ever after.

Or is there? How could there not be?

I love Ayan though I've never met her. I watch her sister
like she may leave me at any moment, disappear
into the light dappling her cheek and just like that

this black couch, this porch strewn with plants,
this dirt-made path we walk smelling of sativa
and turmeric, is an altar to the living and the dead,

is a prayer and an offering.

DONALD DUCK AT THE END OF THE WORLD

My uncle says that one day when it's all over
the sky will be rolled up tight as the blunts
my brother smokes on the front porch
and the dead will be shook from their graves
and sorted according to action.

I am twelve and exhausted from listening,
the small rocks on our porch pinching my thighs.
I know I know already and have games to play
with the boys across the street.

Let God tell it, the end won't come until the trumpets
sound and dajjal pisses and tells the world
it's rain and they believe it. (It's funny
they believe *him* but not when mama says it hurts
here and here and here).

The internet says the word *dajjal* comes
from *dejjel* to gold plate and my mama
the only woman besides God who could tell me to pray
and I'd do it, said the ATMs in Dubai shit gold bricks
and that's how she knew to get my name plate from Sa'udi
where they respect themselves.

During Saturday morning cartoons,
the television showed us the inside of Donald Trump's
mansion in a commercial and his toilet was yup, you guessed it, gold
and I shook my head and said subhanallahhhhhhhh
which is a prayer my uncle would say

I knew from being a good muslim.

But really I knew from watching mama and the way
she got to thumbing and thumbing that ten-dollar bill
that the trumpet might—God forbid—sound
while we were in America pretending to be American
watching Donald Duck
in a vest
shake his fist in a circle.

ACKNOWLEDGMENTS

"Jesus at Wynfield Station" was previously published in *Halal If You Hear Me.*

"What the Living Do" takes its title from the book of poems by Marie Howe.

"Sujui" appears in *Araweelo Abroad* and *The Seventh Wave* in earlier (and different) versions as "Garissa."

In the poem "A Catalog of Fear" Valerie Castile, the mother of Philando Castile, is quoted as saying: "I don't give a fuck what you do. Do what your heart desires . . ." The quote is from a Facebook Live video Ms. Castile recorded on June 17, 2017 after a jury found Officer Yanez not guilty on all charges.

A GIRL IS A SOVEREIGN STATE

JAMILA OSMAN

Published by Akashic Books
©2020 Jamila Osman

ISBN: 978-1-61775-893-5

Akashic Books
Brooklyn, New York, USA
Twitter: @AkashicBooks
Facebook: AkashicBooks
E-mail: info@akashicbooks.com
Website: www.akashicbooks.com

African Poetry Book Fund
Prairie Schooner
University of Nebraska
110 Andrews Hall
Lincoln, Nebraska 68588

TABLE OF CONTENTS

PREFACE
by Ladan Osman

Jamila Osman's *A Girl Is a Sovereign State* is totally sympathetic to contexts outside its own preoccupations. The reader is made sensitive to both its bright and its dim, and is rendered a fellow mourner of all that this gifted poet memorializes. The chapbook opens with "Prayer," and the grief is heavy enough to crack teeth: "I say I miss her and what I mean is / I have carried her ghost a long way." The poem is filled with "warm decay, a splendor." Its speaker collects gifts from her gone sister's cat (dead mice and bird fragments) while speaking into the slippage between what can and can't be grasped, let alone uttered:

> The bird is a gone thing
>
> flying beyond whatever door my sister slipped through
> while I looked the other way.

In the first of many instances throughout this taut collection's gorgeous litany, the speaker, who has "nothing to offer the God of this place," must confront all the faculties and expressions entombed by loss: "How easy," she writes, "to mistake / a symbol for a sign." This is what the living are left to do, our limitations humbling our attempts at eulogy: "What I mean is no one wants to believe / the garden is dying." This poem chases fragments of a portrait; "Prayer" knows it can't carry the missing one's image and doesn't try. It also knows the afterimage is not the image. The speaker is now left to deal with the enormous impression existence makes, and the haunting that is memory. What *does* "gone or going" mean? Several of these poems settle into what happens to those of us left rooted in our bodies while death becomes dynamic, and grieving becomes a new kind of life.

The disquiet resulting from restricted or trauma-thwarted speech is complicated by the desire to belong (if only to survive) or, failing that, recognition of sovereignty. In "English Lessons," tongues "take a new shape." Language is a body within the speaker's body and, if mastered, promises familiarity. "Silence was my first language," the speaker says, and quiet "a rush of water in a season of drought." If quiet is the deluge, which vacuum causes the drought? Is it what exists before language is missed? In "Winter," the speaker's mother, who may be like Jamila's and like my own, arrives in North America with "a phone number in her sweaty palm." A Customs official asks her name and this "girl-mother" answers: *Refugee.* We can guess at her losses, all that she has unloosed to lift her tether and stake it elsewhere: "Her first English word, / an unbirthing." Yes. It's not complicated enough to say a refugee must start anew. Osman's deftness flashes a little humor. Lost in the frenzied violence of naming another "alien" is the refusal to see one's own strangeness, that of course a body sometimes rejects even the lifesaving transplant. The refugee must excise her own experience and rootedness to keep herself intact:

> Only what is unnamed
> can be saved
>
> from the violence
> that surrounds it.

In the next poem "Girls, Girls, Girls," silence in part acts as a protection against rupture and invasion, the disease of bureaucratizing exile: "Before we found the border on the roof of our mouths, / Before the border was English and no one we loved could cross it." Inability to speak or obstinance in speaking is a mausoleum for life, nation, belonging—enshrined as it deserves to be, accessible only to intimates. Many of us have relatives who, after a generation, use English only when forced. "Speak!" the stranger demands, and the one ever-hungry for home resists the sometimes-violence of translation, refusing to make their body a host.

The wordlessness of a survivor appears to be an effect of domination. Every utterance in this chapbook is understood as an insubordination. The redactions in "English Lessons" suggest violations that scorch through speech. But this tongue sears in "Sovereign," where, "The body of a girl / is a nation / with no flag / of its own" and "In Somali freedom / is a word only men know." This is a double exposure of pain, Osman's testimony illuminating what thrives in shadow: a Somali girl is often called stateless, and her body lacks officiality, too. What does it mean to be sovereign but not free? It's a considerable burden for the African woman who too often questions who controls her own and her country's materiality. Yet, this speaker "will not be a stranger / here / or anywhere." In "Wound," the speaker's mother loans her voice:

> I am her only god
> and country, she both
> bloom and break of my heart.

If "The only thing a girl can love without shame is her country," ("Patriots") this speaker has found a haven in the various hellfires a daughter may face.

This realm, which has favored Adam over Eve, is nonetheless "the aftermath of their desire," and "each person is only guilty for what / is lost at their hands." "Original Sin" gives us the incredible image of Eve, or Hawa, as a girl. It's not an easy gift, just as enduring girlhood is not. "Adam is blameless / as all boys will be," she writes, and from this account of his innocence we glean Hawa's, as well as all that isn't available to her. She is at fault "for what has been lost," and the punishment for losing, that Eden is lacking the respite of an earthy garden. This realm pursues her until death, but this imbalance extracts a staggering cost from all humans:

7

Who among us does not suffer
from what Adam forgot?

Unable to tell each other
all that we had wanted,

what we say barely grazes
the surface of what we mean.

This ideology suggests memory is our savior. This could mean an impossible nostalgia drives our human yearning for more than even the beloved rivers and soils of a particular homeland. Jamila Osman's lyric is oriented around a dominion so grand, it only flirts with our feeble imaginations. The speaker and her sister try anyway in "California," and probably almost succeed: "invented our futures" through daydream: ". . . out of the blackness of our skin / and into the wanted blackness of the night . . . stealthy as a people who belonged." Of course, the indigenous don't have to be stealthy unless aggressed. "In Which We Pretend There Was Never a War" suggests that belonging in America is stealing away onto borrowed land, a powerful allusion to the corrupted welcome of the uninvited settler. "No one died for us to meet here, in this land of exiles," the speaker continues in the final poem:

I reach for your hand. Look:
everywhere our bodies touch, a country

where our mothers sing and do not weep.

This is a troubled liberation, not without sadness and broken declarations. There is no exit for the exiled, only quests and more questions, nothing that can cast a shadow larger than our monumental pain. Still, it's worthwhile to search and sing, carrying our aching and the fleeting impacts we make on landscapes and each other.

There's a rare moment of continuity in this box set that reveals the necessity of the African Poetry Book Fund's literary project. In her own chapbook, "Enumeration," Sadia Hassan writes for both Ayan and Jamila Osman:

> I love Ayan though I've never met her. I watch her sister
> like she may leave me at any moment, disappear
> into the light dappling her cheek and just like that
>
> this black couch, this porch strewn with plants,
> this dirt-made path we walk smelling of sativa
> and turmeric, is an altar to the living and the dead,
>
> is a prayer and an offering.
>
> ("What the Living Do")

This is heart-healing documentation of two young Somali poets moving through their paces, sharing space on the page and beyond it.

PRAYER

My sister's cat piles dead things at my feet.
Mice in my shoes, gray and stinking.
Their warm decay, a splendor.

I collect bird parts from the front stoop,
the litter box, the bottom of the stairs.
Soft blade of a beak, underside of a wing,
a paper thin feather.

Once:
a whole bird on the porch,
still slick from the cat's wet mouth,
life pouring out of its body.
Already on its way to where
it is we go from here.

How easy to mistake
a symbol for a sign.

The fragment of the bird is not the bird
or even the memory of the bird.

The bird is a gone thing

flying beyond whatever door
my sister slipped through
while I looked the other way.

I have nothing to offer the God of this place.
A prayer pulls taut as rope between the thing
it asks for and the thing it cannot ask for.

I say I miss her and what I mean is
I have carried her ghost a long way and
what I mean is each of us is gone or going and

what I mean is no one wants to believe
the garden is dying.

ORIGINAL SIN

God gutted Adam,
hauling Hawa from between
his ribs. The first woman coaxed
from the bone of man.

This world is the aftermath of their desire.
The apple rusts the clay of their throats.

To some, Hawa is to blame
for what has been lost.
Adam is blameless
as all boys will be.

On the Day of Judgment
the body will testify against its tenant:
the tongue made to account for
the many languages of its lies.

The eyes will confess every
forbidden glance at salt-mired
cities they could not save.

The green thumb will be apologetic
for every rooted thing it culled
from the earth in envy.

In Islam there is no original sin,
each person is only guilty for what
is lost at their hands.

Before the fall, God taught
Adam the Names of Things.

Words scrolled in the grove
of his mouth, which of them
did he leave behind?

Every word Hawa spoke
is one he remembered.

Who among us does not suffer
from what Adam forgot?

Unable to tell each other
all that we had wanted,

what we say barely grazes
the surface of what we mean.

WINTER

Scene 1:

Location: Toronto Pearson International Airport.
Outside snow softens the unfamiliar landscape, whittles the winter's sharp
    edge.
The Canadian flag flaps in the wind.

Characters: A scowling Customs official in full uniform. A wedding ring
    cutting into his finger.
A young woman with no bags, a slip of paper with a phone number in her
    sweaty palm.

Customs official: *Name?*
My girl-mother: *Refugee.*

End scene.

        Her first English word,
        an unbirthing.

        Only what is unnamed
        can be saved

        from the violence
        that surrounds it.

        Outside the airport
        her lips and knuckles
        split open in the cold.

Everything
in this new world,
a wound.

GIRLS, GIRLS, GIRLS

We were girls once and tragedy was only rumor.

None of our neighbors had been shot dead by the police,
Trayvon Martin's boyish face bore no resemblance to our first crush,
None of us had shut down freeways or bridges in protest.

None of our uncles had been tortured in secret CIA prisons,
No relatives had been disintegrated by drones and called collateral damage,
None of our cousins had perished in refugee camps waiting for paperwork
      to be processed.

No one we knew had been deported,
No one we knew was shivering in a detention center,
None of our people had been lost to the Sonoran Desert,
heat reducing them to teeth scattered in the sand,
No one we loved ever boarded a dinghy only to drown in the salt of the sea.

None of us had ever been spit on waiting in the long lines of Qalandiya,
Nobody's village had been bulldozed, not in Haifa or Jenin, or any of the
lost cities we name our daughters after. Not a single olive tree had been
      uprooted.

We were girls once.

Before the sight of a cop car hollowed the space
in our bellies where we kept our brothers' names.

Before a man became president and we no longer knew who to trust,
Before we learned how many people wanted our parents disappeared.

Before the US went to war with countries we might have been born in,
Before bombs were dropped over cities we might have been raised in,
Before we got our first jobs and our tax dollars massacred people
we might have called neighbors.

Before Nour's mother was murdered by the man she married,
Before our brothers grew up to be like our fathers.

Before strange men called us unfamiliar words as we walked home from
    school,
Before the boys we grew up with slid their fingers up our skirts without our
    permission.

Before we learned enough Arabic to perform the funeral prayer,
Before the first body we mourned was our own.

Before we came to know the geography of our mothers' grief,
Before we contorted our bodies to fill the shape of her lost country.
Before the first time we saw our fathers cry,
Before we tried to be perfect daughters to repent for their sacrifice.

Before we knew there was a border,
Before we looked for the border on a map and could not find it,
Before we found the border on the roof of our mouths,
Before the border was English and no one we loved could cross it.

Before we forgot the language of our parents' grief,
Before we left with only what we could carry on our backs,
Before we returned but found no one who remembered us.

We were girls once

Before girl was synonym for battle or country or ghost.

We are girls still, braids thick as smoke.

Refusing to be martyred before our deaths,
we answer only to the names we choose for ourselves

SOVEREIGN

The body of a girl
is a nation

with no flag
of its own.

Its borders slick
as the oil in her hair.

In Somali freedom
is a word only men know.

In English freedom
is the sound a gun makes

as it loosens a bullet
from its barrel.

A girl is a sovereign state.

I will not be a stranger
here or   anywhere.

ENGLISH LESSONS

We learned English faster than our parents, their tongues
too old to take a new shape. Our tongues still coated in milk.
This meant we didn't pray like they did. God didn't answer when we called.
English teachers *tsked tsked tsked* when our words lost letters:
when ending became endin became the end.

English was a world we built with our small hands.
Our small brown hands. I was a girl and nothing
belonged to me except what came out of this mouth of mine.

When my cousin put his [   ] in my [   ], and when my uncle
[   ]ed me in the living room of my home as my parents ate dinner
in the next room, and when a strange man grabbed my [   ] on the
    train
the summer of my senior year, and when and when and when and when
    and when,
I wanted to say stop but didn't know what language to say it in.

In Somalia we speak Somali, in America we speak English,
or we speak nothing at all.

All the women I know speak in whispers.
When I try and tell some stories language turns to iron,
heavy and rusting in the back of my throat.
I bite my tongue and taste blood.

Silence was my first language.
I am fluent in its cadences.
I know quiet is a celebration,

the way it pours out of a mouth.
A rush of water in a season of drought.

THE FEMALE OF THE SPECIES

The African elephant
has no natural predators.

Calves who cannot rely
on size for safety may fall prey
to lions or hyenas.

Across species childhood
is a game of dumb luck.

The elephant's most formidable
enemy is the iron lust of the hunter.
His cocked rifle, his tinny greed.

How he reduces a body
to what it yields. Tusks whittled
to billiard balls, piano keys,
ornate necklaces.

Hacked incisors siphoned
from skull, clumps of tissue
and exposed nerve.

Blood gasping from a wound,
no mercy to levee the gusts.

The matriarch asks the herd
to see with her wizened eyes.

The carcasses rusting
in the copper of the bush.
The receding river of her kin.

Oh, female of the human species,
you need no convincing of the cruelty
of the hunter's hands.

You have been the darting
target of his desire.

The well in the field
of his brimming thirst.

King of your animal body,
how he thrills in the sport
of your flesh.

Sweat stiffening your hide,
fear swelling the black
of your pupils.

Salt of your teeth
whittled to silence.

Throat full of blood
and no words.

WOUND
(IN THE VOICE OF MY MOTHER)

No doctor
could dam the bleeding.

Not an omen but a daughter
born in a river of blood.

Red of the autumn
leaf's descent. Red
of my body's sea.

No holy man could clear
a path for her,

my rabid miracle,
child turned lamb at the feet
of Abraham's piety.

I am her only god
and country, she both
bloom and break of my heart.

Jekyll of no nation,
she is nowhere
I know.

Nowhere
I've been before.

CALIFORNIA

We first drove across
the Golden Gate Bridge at sunset.

Awed to silence at its tawny magnitude,
even the baby blinked in wonder.

My sister and I invented our futures
in the back seat of that minivan.

Imagined ourselves out of the blackness of our skin
and into the wanted blackness of the night.

Two girls unwed to reason, we vowed
to move to San Francisco as soon as we were old enough.

Aabo drove all night to get us home.
The radio a soft hum out of the mouth of the speaker.

We crossed from California into Oregon
stealthy as a people who belonged.

In the dark it was not possible to tell
where one state ended and the other began.

The roiling hills unbeholden
to the strange markings of maps.

On that trip there was no such thing as America.
Only a bridge that seemed to hold up the sky,

only the joy that came from knowing
what would meet us on the other side.

PATRIOTS

The first time I go home the water makes me sick. I am trapped in a cloud of wet heat. The mosquitoes are blood mad. Men at the market look at me with a similar hunger. They call me American Girl. I feel a mountain level in my chest. I name its peak desire. Longing makes me violent. I want to hurt the American Girl inside me. I want to rip her tongue from my mouth. Undo the dumb silence of her birth. All my languages are borrowed or stolen. I am not sure what the difference is anymore. Some days I am not a girl, but a house made of all the wrong words. I peel language back from the walls like paint. What is left? A home or only the myth of one? A girl or only her shadow? In the evenings my sister and I sit on Ayeeyo's porch listening to the radio. The sky's pink tongue lolls over our small heads. The only Somali song we know the words to is the national anthem. We sing as loud as we can and beam with the sheen of belonging. We get all the words right. No one tells us to be quiet. The only thing a girl can love without shame is her country.

IN THE VOICE OF THE MAD MULLAH
GUUL AMA GEERI // VICTORY OR DEATH

Soldiers of the Sufi Order,
baptized in blood, holy water of revolution.

No sins to atone for,
not ours or our fathers.

Dervishes milking freedom
from stone, reckless in devotion,
whirling whirling whirling

towards a freedom
we only knew in scripture.

Refusing to be shriveled by history,
our language loosened string
in the harp of our children's mouths.

I knew what our fathers had survived,
heard rumors of all they had not.

We were innocent when the war started,
men when it was over.

IN WHICH WE PRETEND THERE WAS NEVER A WAR

Holy kingdom of hash and sweat,
muadhin crowing in the distance,
the world made in just six days.

Whose God do you pray to
when fear buckles your knees?
What name sterns your bowed mouth?

Light from the minaret pierces the sky,
waning gibbous, a poet's favorite metaphor.
I squint and it is small enough to fit in my pocket.

If we try we can pretend we are anywhere
but here. Our people have never known catastrophe.
No one died for us to meet here, in this land of exiles,

on these streets lined with what our fathers could not utter,
not in any language of their departure or arrival.

Soldiers fire tear gas into crowds of unarmed civilians.
The gas becomes a balloon animal puffed to brilliance
above the heads of small children.

Martyrs bloat to life. A storm of bullets spin
back towards the mouth of their sin, ants unfollowing
a trail of crumbs.

We are not the victims of this war, nor the children
of its consequence. There is no blood on our hands,

only the pale red light of evening.
You pass me a cigarette and I inhale,
orbed end sun of our chosen sky.

This is all we know of fire.
All we know of smoke.

Let me pretend this love is fate,
an accident unmarred by the bright
wound of our histories.

I reach for your hand. Look:
everywhere our bodies touch, a country

where our mothers sing and do not weep.

ACKNOWLEDGMENTS

An earlier version of "English Lessons" was published in *Brevity*.

Earlier versions of "Original Sin" and "English Lessons" were published as part of the Brunel International Poetry Prize.

The line "no one wants to believe the garden is dying" in the poem "Prayer" is from the Forugh Farrokhzad poem "I Pity the Garden."

A MOUTHFUL OF HOME
TRYPHENA YEBOAH

This is a work of fiction. All names, characters, places, and incidents are a product of the author's imagination. Any resemblance to real events or persons, living or dead, is entirely coincidental.

Published by Akashic Books
©2020 Tryphena Yeboah

ISBN: 978-1-61775-885-0

Akashic Books
Brooklyn, New York, USA
Twitter: @AkashicBooks
Facebook: AkashicBooks
E-mail: info@akashicbooks.com
Website: www.akashicbooks.com

African Poetry Book Fund
Prairie Schooner
University of Nebraska
110 Andrews Hall
Lincoln, Nebraska 68588

For my father, of course

TABLE OF CONTENTS

PREFACE
by Lauren K. Alleyne

The poems in Tryphena Yeboah's collection, *A Mouthful of Home,* are visceral. They are a raw, stunning articulation of what it means to live in the world with a sense of self that is both damaged and resilient. They reside at the intersection of faith and despair, loss and hope, wound and healing, as shown in "I, Too, Have Been Trying to Exist in My Own Body":

> I—belong—here. Faith wears out my knees
> but I never stop walking.
> Every morning by stepping out these doors,
> I have already won one too many wars.

Throughout the collection the body is refracted again and again as the speaker wrestles with her fundamental mortality in an exquisite disquisition on the body and its frailty. Illness is one lens through which the body is refracted in "You Think Every Door Swings Open for You," as the speaker seeks to make sense of her father's decline, "the cancer having eaten him to the bone," and his ultimate death.

Surrender and denial of the body are examined through the speaker's mother, who at one point, in "A God of Ash," "swings with the Holy Spirit" and in "And What If I Breathe Out" tries to convince her daughter that the body is immaterial—"we're already unseen." Even the mother's face, which haunts the speaker's mirror as she regards her own, brings to the fore the question of whether the body belongs to us. In addition to its vulnerability to personal violation, disease, and possession, the body is also presented as vulnerable to social violence. In "Possible Terror Attack, Churches Targeted," Yeboah writes of bodies razed to nothingness in "an unholy explosion," and, in "The Body as Proof," she elegizes "three missing girls," describing their possible ends as mutilated and degraded bodies. All of this serves to remind us that we are all walking graveyards, our deaths already scripted into our bodies.

Beating like a small heart throughout *A Mouthful of Home* and undergirding the poems' searching and poignant inquiry, is the wrenching question, *What do I do with my rape?* What we learn is that there is no single answer. Some days its reverberation is physical: the speaker "can barely breathe"; other days bring the wearying story of survival. "Reporting Abuse" describes a sense of being "a broken thing that somehow made it out alive." Most often these two states are intertwined and overwhelming as we see in the poem "I Tell My Mother I Want a Body That Expands":

> And so when my mother walks into my room, finds me curled
> on the floor, I say without turning to look at her: I know we need
> a knife to pull out a knife but today, meet me with gentleness. If
> there's a language for a woman learning to breathe, I'm speaking
> it—even if my voice is just a whisper.

It is this intertwining, intersecting refusal to claim victory or defeat that is the true triumph of this collection. These poems walk us through mindscapes sculpted by trauma—the quicksand of memory, the stubborn ruins of faith, the grinding self-doubt, the distrust of and deep desire for joy. They are testimony to the force of will and insistence on one's right to exist that such survival demands.

Here, then, are poems that remind us of the multifaceted, hyperdimensional nature of our being; poems that condense our vastness, telling us that "all of life is a waiting room." But they also expand us beyond any knowing, saying in "Honoring What My Family Will Never Know," "we're made of more rooms / than we can count." Here are poems that invite us to sit with the complexity of our always-imperiled bodies and existences—"tomorrow / is an emergency exit and we don't always / make it out alive"—and instruct us in their abundance in "I Sing Therefore We Sing": "joy that is shared never runs out and my hands stay open." Here is the inhale, the exhale, the labor of each drawn breath, and the miraculous risk/risky miracle of living.

I AM NOTHING IF I CAN'T BREATHE JOY

When suffering knocks at your door and you say there is no seat for him, he tells you not to worry because he has brought his own stool.

—Chinua Achebe

It should be difficult to build a home because you want it to last. My body breaks after every storm and I'm dying to know how far I must go to find a peace that wouldn't be taken away from me. Every day I forget how to say my name a little and I blame the heavens. God has a way of making dead things look like a blessing but faith is locked tight out of me. By that I mean, I want to see things first before I name them. Not the shadow of things. Not the shape of things. If I put a face to sadness, it is because I have known it, touched it, become one with it. If I call a man a fire, it is because I have been burned before. I have a voice and when I speak, people only remember the stammering and forget the words. If I could do one thing differently, I would like to say my name without tremble; feel it leave my lips with power, taste the fear and still speak. I understand I am a sad poet. I carry grief in the words and do not apologize for the tears. Every recital is a grave that opens up and someone dies. They say what else can you say about a home than its darkness and have you tried writing a poem about your mother without making it heavy. I say my mind is a forest and when I strike a match, everything burns, even the memories, even my father's laugh. I save nothing from the fire yet everything stays with me, even the memories, even my father's laugh. I am nothing if I can't breathe a joy that only I understand. An emotion which isn't shared does not cease to exist. I am most known for my premature birth of things—a love which isn't ready, an unsure forgiveness, a wound still learning to heal. Believe me when I say I'm dying to know how far I must go to find a peace that isn't taken away from me. It should be difficult to build a home because you want it to last but my body, it washes up the shore after every storm—half-naked, half-dead. And even then, it learns to dance.

WE KEPT OUR HANDS UP, IN PRAYER AND IN SURRENDER

In this house, we have no songs, only silence.
Mother, the only one who sees God, makes soup
like she is revisiting an old poem.
Kitchen walls are covered by recipes, cursive handwriting
fading every day on brown paper.
Father remains seated in a rusty wheelchair by the door,
a newspaper from 1995 on his lap.
He tells me that's the year I was born,
tells me he had known no famine like that time.
Tells me he reads the story to remember there was
a time of lack, of hunger
and in his remembrance, there is gratitude.
I say you don't always have to visit the past to be thankful.
And he responds, how will you know how far you've come?
What do you have to measure?
You only know you've come through waters if the water is behind you.
And you only appreciate land when you remember
your legs almost broke under the sea.
The stroke has us all taking turns to look after him.
One Sunday, on my brother's watch, was when the seizure began.
A nine-year-old dreamy boy ran from the house screaming.
Mother only had to add one more spice to her soup,
stirring with her steady hands, yelling at my brother for
banging the door.
And I watched from the doorway, my knees buckling
underneath my trembling body.
Everything happened quickly after that—
Mother throwing off her apron and running to his side,

my brother peeping through a window—
all three of us weeping without realizing.
And mother, praying, lifting up her hands

MY BODY, HAVING LEARNED RESURRECTION

The day ripens on my face.
The opening of my eyes is the plucking of stars
and I want to keep the glistening thing forever
but my hands, I need them empty to carry other dreams like
pulling myself out of bed,
washing my face and carving today's date into walls
as another triumphant exit from death, numbness—
the crashing state of absence from the here and now.
Suppose you enter a room to find me sitting across a window
looking into tomorrow,
will you touch me on the shoulder to wake me up
or bring me closer to you to feed your loneliness?
Suppose instead of turning my neck to face you
I crawl out of the window and run towards the light,
will you follow me not knowing where I'm going or
will you pull me back by the arm, dragging me back to yourself?
My heart shall keep its promise of staying soft and open.
I'm versed inside a language that demands that before I speak,
I weigh the words on my tongue. Must be salt, must be water.
Everyone speaks of never returning to the places that almost drowned them.
Meanwhile, I am a girl moved by the shape of scars.
If I want to know how a wound made a home out of me,
does it mean I enjoyed the pain?
I want the joy of healing pulsing close to my skin
My body, having learned resurrection, more tender than before.
I want a tangible appreciation of life.
I stretch my hand and the day is a fruit I bite into,
a kind of sweetness I can wear without growing tired;
a cascading joy enough to keep me believing that no door is an accident.
You walk through some only to meet yourself.

I TELL MY MOTHER I WANT A BODY THAT EXPANDS

Into a map. She wants to know where I'll travel to. I say "myself." Some days I loosen the folds on my arm and I call myself a surgeon/ take out a piece from my belly, widen my hips. A mirror can have different names: a dream, a boxing ring, a mother's undeniable satisfaction. I am neither of these but somehow I wake up in the middle of the night, parts of my face swollen from hunger and my mother looking at me and saying, "you remind me of when your father was a good man." I was named after the memory of hope, the longing of a lover's return. This should explain my opening of doors, my waiting, my unreasonable patience for boys who choose to take their time in wanting me. I want to trust my past to lead me where I don't have to choose between being alive and slicing myself in half. These days, nothing fits into my mouth like the trauma. I hold it in my teeth like a trophy begging to be seen. I can fix the puzzle of my face better than I can take down my depression. And so when my mother walks into my room, finds me curled on the floor, I say without turning to look at her: I know we need a knife to pull out a knife but today, meet me with gentleness. If there's a language for a woman learning to breathe, I'm speaking it—even if my voice is just a whisper.

AT CHURCH, I WATCH MY MOTHER
DANCE THE CANCER AWAY

. . . come celebrate
with me that everyday
something has tried to kill me
and has failed.
               —Lucille Clifton

throws her hands up as if to tell us she needs more saving than all of us
she turns and turns and I grow dizzy watching her white knitted dress
transform into a fast ghost I can never catch up with
I hear the kids in the pew behind me giggling
they must be thinking—what a crazy woman.
look, she doesn't know what to do to herself
it infuriates me that they misunderstand the coping mechanism of a widow
that a woman who loses her lover should sit at the back of the church,
shaking and weeping in her little black dress
having prayers passed to her like a meal no one would eat
it kills me that she is expected to grieve well,
take sympathy like a love offering and soak her breaking heart inside
I want to shut the mouths of these kids
tape mother's favorite Bible verses over their lips
and teach them silence.
despite myself, even mourning feels light after a while
no one walks the earth burying their whole selves after a loss,
only small parts—little by little
I know mother has long buried the loneliness of her nights,
weeping eyes and even her songs
if I have to watch every step of this dance,
even as it fades into the ground, I'll take it.

14

grief, after all, only prepares us for more grief
and strength is that which falls but does not break.

I, TOO, HAVE BEEN TRYING TO EXIST IN MY OWN BODY

I wash my throat with mother's promises and speak with choking:
I—belong—here. Faith wears out my knees
but I never stop walking.
Every morning by stepping out these doors,
I have already won one too many wars.
My fears have me in chains.

If I say too much, the world will spit on my truth.
If I laugh too much, my joy will be taken away from me.
I've been too quiet for a woman alive in this time.
I spend each moment asking "when will this end?

This fear of becoming, of growing out of myself,
of stretching and stretching?"
I did not come all this way
—waking up, dragging my feet on the cold floor
which has threatened to open up and swallow me,
washing away bad dreams from my face,
planting a song in my lungs—only to die.

I hold the gate open for myself,
inhale and exhale. I grab the arm of the day
and our fingers touch. Oh what small comforts
lie ahead, what blessing. Now tell me,
what storm shall come our way
that we won't overcome.

I SING THEREFORE WE SING

I need you to understand:
my joy is something you can wear, too.
Throw it over your head like a blessing bestowed,
keep it wrapped around your body in the cold nights.
In your loneliness, I am there. Warmth is love.
Love is as open as the mouth of God and we can both feast.
A big table only means I have more food for myself and you, too,
and asks why do you sit so far away? Pull up a chair.
Bitterness scratches its body till it's sore.
Walks around the room pointing at everything
it wished it owned. As if two hearts couldn't leap
over the joy of one and two voices in an empty room
were incapable of making music. As if, should I begin to grow
out of myself, my stretched hands wouldn't make your loneliness
lose its name. I say this with love:
a joy that is shared never runs out and my hands stay open.

YOU THINK EVERY DOOR SWINGS OPEN FOR YOU

But not always. Some stay closed even as you try to push them down. Mother says a door is a wall with hope and what lays on the other side can change your life forever. I believe her. When my father grew ill, the cancer having eaten him to the bone, they carried him into the guest room where he stayed until his last breath. My brothers and I were never allowed in. Some nights I curled myself by the door and listened for anything. I heard whimpering, slow heavy breaths. Once I think I heard father weep. All I could think of was moving past this border into his sacred space and into his strong arms. When I mentioned it to mother, a cloud of sadness hovered over her face. She asked, "What if his arms are not strong to hold you? What will you do then?" Sit on his lap, I said. "And what if his knees are weak and they'll break under your weight?" Then he can sit on mine. Mother laughed and that was all the ticket I needed. One night in August, I crawled in the dark across the hall to the guest room. I turned the knob and poked my small head inside. Father laid on the bed breathing lightly. There were pills on the table, more than I could count. There was food he hadn't eaten from the previous day. And an open Bible on his chest. He didn't turn but asked, "Who?" and his voice was so faint I nearly missed it. It's me, Papa, I said, still behind the door, my neck stretched. I must have stood there waiting for an invitation because Papa seemed to be filled with a somewhat shock, as he replied, "No, no, my baby. Go back. Go back." And of course, I ran.

A GOD OF ASH

At home, we break the silence with a prayer.
You can find here two boys searching for

answers. A widow who forgets to feed her children
but remembers to sing. And a girl who slices the

emptiness in half to see herself. The rooms in this
house are filled with weeping but we will not grieve

forever. I am not afraid of feeling sadness. I am afraid
of carrying it around for so long it almost becomes a

part of me. Mother swings with the Holy Spirit at her
hip. The memory of my father writhing in pain is as

clear as a white sky. But mother, she sings: *joy like
a river, joy like a river, joy like a river in my soul.*

I choke back tears. Faith is all we know. If we could,
we would walk through the fire blindfolded and name our

burnt bodies the will of God. But what God takes delight
in ash? Watches the flames spread wild over everything

and tells us to trust?

HONORING WHAT MY FAMILY WILL NEVER KNOW

Leaving opens us up,
makes a keeper out of us,
shows us we're made of more rooms
than we can count.
Kisses us on the hand and holds on too tight.
We speak of love like it is a garment,
wrap it around the body like a promise.
There are days words like *hope* are trapped
between our teeth because to us, tomorrow
is an emergency exit and we don't always
make it out alive.
I live in the telling of stories that endure
the brutality of truth:
One Sunday, I remember sitting at my father's feet
and looking up at his face—a beam of light.
In a whisper, he said, "I won't be here forever"
and I threw my head back and laughed;
without a clue this sentence will someday turn
into a noose that tightens about my throat.
I laughed and my innocence bared its teeth at me.

A little girl plays with fire because her father lit
the match. Nothing from fathers burns.

WHERE THE BODY HAS BEEN

No one knows.
Somewhere my mother is flipping through my diary
circling words like *lonely, heart and mother.*

i My lonely is an open mouth. I swallow myself again and again
ii I am terrified by how much pain my heart can bear
iii Some mothers are gifts we're not quite sure what to do with,
how to keep, how to make ours

What I call secret is no longer a language barrier.
People will make of your truths what they want
and what is permission to a chorus of words that
only speak for itself?
The world has been to me a fighting ring where
I have learned to fight with fists and hope is a wound
which goes after better things than pain.
The world has been to me a fast dance
where I've spun myself dizzy,
found love that was hard and sweet and clung to it.
The world has been to me a funeral ground where
I have buried precious things—
my father's voice under the earth,
his blue shirt rotting away in the dirt.

THE BODY AS PROOF

On the TV, the faces of the three girls missing are a blur,
they've been gone for sixty days and a woman
shown rolling on the floor, wailing,
can only be one of the mothers.
The journalist, unsure about what to do next, kneels
beside her and pushes the microphone to her mouth.
Sometimes, in bringing out the news, throats must
be cut open where they've been shut for good.
"What would you like to say to the government?"
The woman is barely moving now, her eyes
caught dead on camera, a shallow sound, a loud emptiness.
Absence from the body is death
and a grieving mother is more at peace knowing
their child is dead than not knowing at all.
A half-eaten body is consolation.
A body returned by the mouth of the sea is consolation.
A body with parts missing is consolation.
We give everything as proof of death to replace
having to attend burials in our minds for the rest
of our lives—graveyards everywhere we look.

REPORTING ABUSE

The way to get out of some kind of pain is to,
with your whole body, crawl out of the wound.

A journalist speaks to me in a rehearsed tone—
tell me how it happened. You can take your time, she says.

(You can take your microphone back to when I needed to be heard).
(You can take your lights back to when it was just the darkness and I—
and a stranger's hand on my back).

I say I do not want to talk about it.

I read the question in her eyes faster than my skirt was stripped off that night:
what will you do with your rape?

How about you leave my thighs to heal,
leave my voice to learn to speak without trembling.

How about I find the thin line between a man wanting to harm me
while hungry for my body and a man wanting to love me while
longing for my heart.

How about you give me peace. Give me time.
Give these scars a place to breathe.

All of life is a waiting room and I'm finding that sometimes
I am the emergency and I have no good news.

I believe things stay dead for a reason so please let me mourn.

Let me grieve. Let me bring flowers to the parts of me that died
and let me remember the cold nights. Let me remember to close my eyes
and hold my (own) hand.

What do I do with my rape?
I keep it warm, under blankets. I hide every sharp object and
when I'm with a man, my body turns to water that can drown both of us.
When I'm with a man, I'm a fighter and then, a lover.

You want a story. A survivor. A broken thing that somehow made it out alive
and I, I only want to live.

NOW I DO NOT EVEN LOOK AT THE SKY*

One can only hope that a girl grows old with her father and that he ages but not too much.

Grows a wrinkled skin that can still play in the sand. Strong legs that will never be taken away from him because a girl loves to run with the man who raised her. I'll tell you what I know about the fatherless: They're a fractured and a whole at the same time. I was born in conflict. As my mother gave life, my father took it away. I do not know what is more strange- that life and death happen in the same space or that the two can exist side by side and no one can tell the difference. Cancer is a rough language. Rolls off the tongue like a curse. Rotten. The more you listen, the more your heart shrinks. He breathed still. Even smiled a little. But I tell people I watched my father die slowly every day. I know because I buried the old parts of him. Dug the wet earth and buried his strength, with my brothers holding him on their shoulders. Dug the wet earth and buried his laugh, the only sound he was making were whimpers, songs of agony. Dug the wet earth and buried his memories, he forgot my name, called his wife Salma, thought my brothers were men of God. Dug the wet earth and buried his hope, he wouldn't get up from the hospital bed, wouldn't eat, wouldn't look at us. A daughter should live this life escaping into the arms of her father. But here I am, in and out of existence, holding on to hands that have long disappeared. I too, have started to lose parts of myself. It's true that the death of a loved one is the death of many parts of ourselves. Even more, the deaths of our whole selves. I wake up, numb to everything. I know the end of me is here when I can't feel the wind on my face. I keep the doors locked, the windows shut. God is still God but I will not look at the sky today.

Title from Nadezhda Mandelstam's last letter to her husband.

POSSIBLE TERROR ATTACK, CHURCHES TARGETED

And so I pray with one eye open.
Raise my hands in worship but not high enough.
Sit at the pew by the door, tell the usher
"might run out for an emergency"
And by that I mean, an unholy explosion.
And by that I mean the communion table turned upside down.
And the only bread to be broken will be our bodies, our blood as wine.
The cross collapses unto a pregnant woman clutching her Bible
between her breasts. Who will save us now? Even though we walk
in the valley of the shadow of death,
we do fear the evil of men. Our God is with me but a bullet sits inside of us.
Surely, goodness and mercies shall follow us but this is death
and what if we want a life that runs over? What if we want to carry the cross
and our babies at our backs? My hiding place, where in You can I fold
myself in two—become small, become invisible, slowly diminish into a faith
that walks on water only when you're near. Where in You does this moment
become a fire that doesn't burn because You're here?

THE HANDS THAT SEIZED YOUR JOY ARE EMPTY

And so now, laugh. Head thrown back,
count every blessing you've ever disowned
and make it yours. Why do we tear ourselves
away from good things? Are we not deserving?
Even the sky stays open for us.
God stands in the portrait where the flames burn down
everything and leaves my heart. I watch his throne melt along
with my skin and I think: maybe this is the end of life.
Why does He not quench the fire?
Why does He not swallow the flames?
Why does He watch the collapse of things He's built
with His hands?
I want waters but He holds me so I'm filled.
I want peace but He holds me so I'm filled.
I want deliverance but He holds me so I'm filled.
The blessing, it is only one and so I count it,
and even if I burn, I'm more alive than I've ever been,
my hope bursting from the seams of a life well loved.

AND WHAT IF I BREATHE OUT

My mother wants to shrink, make my body look smaller in a skirt. Says it has nothing to do with rape. Says a woman does not have to fold herself to be invisible. Says we're already unseen—even when we're loud, even when we're the brightest in the room. Says a woman's body should fit in the dress it was made for. I believe her. But she bites off my size, spits it out when I'm not looking. Says "here, try this." Too small, I say. *What if you breathe in, tuck your belly in like a secret. Zip it up from the back and no one will ever know.* I don't know what's sadder—that my ribs are squeezed and I can barely breathe or that I have to keep secret my own skin. To wash away my very existence as though the world hasn't spent years trying to make me disappear.

MEASUREMENT OF HOLY

HOLY

NADRA MABROUK

Published by Akashic Books
©2020 Nadra Mabrouk

ISBN: 978-1-61775-884-3

Akashic Books
Brooklyn, New York, USA
Twitter: @AkashicBooks
Facebook: AkashicBooks
E-mail: info@akashicbooks.com
Website: www.akashicbooks.com

African Poetry Book Fund
Prairie Schooner
University of Nebraska
110 Andrews Hall
Lincoln, Nebraska 68588

TABLE OF CONTENTS

PREFACE
by Karen McCarthy Woolf

Nadra Mabrouk's *Measurement of Holy* is an intrinsically ambitious work, for how do we come to measure such things as holiness? If a poet has any official, vocational remit, then this attempted activity might encapsulate the endeavor, and it's one which Mabrouk makes her own as a citizen of the twenty-first century. And if, as the opening poem, "The Condition," makes clear, we are to write poems in a time when "the world ends around you, / earth tearing root by root," and "horses / stagger into holes, / neighing into the darkness," then the poet's job is most likely situated somewhere among spiritual cartographer, ecological activist, and, in this case, a poultry trader's traveling daughter. It is under such specific conditions that these poems of sacred and domestic ecologies play out—as an elegantly woven gossamer of everyday detail and, on occasion, as larger archetypes, such as Israfil, the Islamic angel of music, who sounds his horn as the day of judgment approaches.

Born in Egypt, Mabrouk's family left for the United States when she was seven. If she is a creature of measurement, it is the distance between the home of childhood and a diasporic adult experience that she evaluates. This sense of scale materializes literally in poems such as "Smallness," where seemingly insignificant aspects of daily life, here set in a café called Routine, are juxtaposed against a more urgent landscape, where the "sky is a gorged fig" and the "nearly bare" birches recall Frost's. Yet in Mabrouk's poem—written in our technologized era fraught with ever-increasing global complexities—instead of an imagined, aspirational innocence of swinging playfully from branches, "the children are running covered in smoke."

Elsewhere in the collection, as in "Morning on Bedford Avenue," this capacity to capture the quotidian and transform it into a larger, more resonant moment manifests through closely observed metaphor, which builds throughout the book. As such, an almost anecdotal narrative about the speaker's sister leaving an apartment for the day—or forever—is both anchored and destabilized by the rendition of that departure, in which "someone / is singing about getting it right / this time. She puts her coffee in the fridge. / The refrain is dripping from her teeth."

Refrain as a litany of separation and by extension loss is a syntactical strategy Mabrouk deploys to significant effect. While "Brother as a Younger Self, Humming" draws on a tradition of literary portraiture, it is also a paean to music itself, where three Mohameds—Fouad, Mohy, and Fawzi—become four in the "shimmering corner" of their grandmother's balcony. "Father as Adolescent, Smoking" is also a work of memoir, although "in this memory"—a phrase that repeats throughout the poem as a mesmeric incantation—we meet the teenager who existed before the daughter was conceived. It is a cinematic scene, a quality that infuses many of the book's poignant vignettes, which flickers across the page, accurate yet dreamlike in its intensity:

> and your own body, stifled by cotton,
> by the ash already starting to spit out
> its gray teeth in your lungs,
> smoking behind the market again, sun-bent
> fingers twitching like dust trying to forget

In a May 2019 interview published online on *Africa in Dialogue* with the South African writer Nkateko Masinga, Mabrouk, who has lived in many different locations, articulates the poetics of embodiment, saying, "I have held on to so many places in my body, and they often appear in my dreams. I have known impermanence for the longest time." It is in this way that life experience via familial recollection seeps in—around the edges and radiating out through the center of the poems, as dust illumined in the sun, as works of both intimate and cultural witness. In "For the Bagged Body in Front of Koshary Ameen Restaurant," for example, she identifies both a "stubbornness to grief" and the fragilities of the physical and of relationships—between father and daughter, between the unidentified corpse in the zipped-up body bag and the world.

The very first words spoken in "Autumn, Spiraling" are by the poet's mother, who is later remembered "on the phone" upset that her daughter recalls her in the kitchen plucking geese, "their necks hanging over her wrists / like unclasped bracelets." It is bejeweled similes such as these that make Mabrouk's poems irresistibly quotable: the feast is right there on the table before the reader, unfolding its lyric complexities.

Mabrouk's shifting landscape is one where food is always more than simple sustenance: it is the bread that is broken, the sheep that is sacrificed; it is a conduit through which some of that process of measurement may take place. In this manner, the central matrilineal relationship unfolds, almost unceremoniously, as "a wound clothed / in a faithful hum / to make its worth and weight / some small measurement of holy" ("Mother as Goat Bone, Wrapped in Aluminum").

THE CONDITION

My Mother tells me
that God says
even if, even while,
the world ends around you,
earth tearing root by root,
even while the horses
stagger into holes,
neighing into the darkness,
filling their mouths
to the throat,
when the horn sounds off,
Israfil balancing his clouded
weight on a rock,
his lips cracking and gold,
even while you hear
the ghosts leaving the spines,
their hair longer than ever,
breaths coming out
in timed instruments,
even while the waters
seethe open,
bodies rolling to the shore.

If there is a seed
in your palm,
you must bend to the soil
and plant it.

AUTUMN, SPIRALING

The spine is a string of pearls,
my doctor says, lower it carefully
on the table, each pearl
equally distanced, immaculate
centered failure. At some point in life
you have to learn what type of runner you are
and I have learned I prefer stumbling
into the bone-cage of landscape,
hands fanned open to the recursive.
There is a kindred to healing, everyone
in a violet, ancient line, the occasional
sound of twigs snapping as we move
into our desired symmetry,
the round-mouthed snap of silence.
I am no different, trying to return
to some acoustic-breathed meadow,
tired of burrowing backward
into the signal. My mother on the phone
is upset that I still remember her sitting
on the kitchen floor of her mother's
apartment in Shobra, plucking feathers
from the mottled bodies of geese, their insides
jeweled and engorged on their own shimmering,
their necks hanging over her wrists
like unclasped bracelets.

SMALLNESS

We are sitting outside the café Routine,
named after this dailiness, mechanics.
The birches are nearly bare.
The children are running covered in smoke.
The cup does not warm me anymore.
A father passes by with a sobbing ghost,
tells it, *"You know what you do when the winds
come like that? You make yourself smaller."*
The sky is a gorged fig, October
is fog-wrapped and urgent.
No one notices us anymore, how we barely talk,
how we succumb to the ferocity of air,
still swollen with dumb pride, unforgiven.

FOR THE BAGGED BODY IN FRONT OF KOSHARY AMEEN RESTAURANT

Sometimes, I think about your hair, how it must have smelled of the space in bones where and when we curve inward, layered in casein, dry oats, incoherences. How yesterday, you picked up a slab of sheep meat, a couple of rib bones for dinner tonight, tomatoes. How yesterday, you might have forgotten to soothe yourself in forgiveness and the temporary bleached wave of gratitude, its constant bell. There is a stubbornness to grief. Its crooked stem continues to hang at an angle from the clay. My father and I stood on the corner of Emad El-Deen Street, stared at how you were wrapped in your bag for hours because you didn't have any ID on you, how a name must still be somewhere, starting to cloud in someone's mouth. My father was pressing on to my hand, as though the smaller the space between our fingers, the more certain we would become of our own bodies: the bitter promise of calcified bones, brief blades the dusky color of iron, derma folding into its stretch, everything beneath fluttering, contained.

LAST NIGHT I WAS A MOTH'S WIDTH RUNNING THROUGH THE STREETS

I am a tired child in Cairo again, flitting between the angry drivers and my mother is holding my hand like a fine-haired braid, *do not apologize for frailty but you need to eat more; your stomach is thinning, soon you won't be able to hold anything.* My insides yawn into one another in the heat's tender and closed fist, blinking bumper to bumper, car sealants: glittering saliva in their paint-stamped paths. This afternoon's route home is familiar— my legs are already splintering into halves then quarters, I don't have the energy to keep up. I missed breakfast this morning, a thread of blood elongating inside the bowl after she broke the egg. I missed breakfast this morning, holding a stomach like a failing engine, imagine it sputtering on the damp air that must be held inside the body, the lack of something fuller to flood. We are late. I am holding her back. The drivers' heads are throbbing with stiffening veins, more blood jelling in its slowing movement—days-old animal bones wrapped in plastic, guava at the bottoms of the drawers. I try to walk faster. My mother's voice never-ending, pulled long and taut in the afternoon, a skin thinning in its stretch, exhausted of all it encompasses.

ON NOT PRAYING IN TWO YEARS

Someone ended up inside the stomach of a whale covered in the wrung sinews
of the day before any breaches of light.

I forget the name of the swallowed, and think about the rumen instead, how you
can swallow a prey whole, hair trailing after in its wet

acrylic movement, back against the lurid wall, listening to the echoing
container of the heart until it drowns.

My mother tells me to say God's name every day, but the air lately is a stillborn
with one last hot cry in its mouth.

Trapped in the numbered joints, I succumb to what falls but still think about the
    history
of redundancies, how the whale song travels

through centuries of bones and still sounds just as newly-haunted. In the dream,
I give birth to a girl, then get up

and search for her down the momentary hallways, everyone walking past me like a
    myth.
I said I don't understand silence,

and I am always looking for a familiar face, how your chest flutters seraphic, yet
still terrene and unforgiving.

I say many things instead of a name lately: territory of depleted seabeds. shoulder
blades curled in whittled roundedness. Someone is bent over mud, looking for
water. There is always blood where a room should be now. I am diminishing.

MORNING ON BEDFORD AVENUE

My sister takes few things with her
before leaving—bone comb
with baby hairs at the edges, wooden
pocket mirror, last night's meat
folded in plastic.
Her cheek is stained, a smeared
glistening on each bone, silver
curling the beginning and end
to each eyelid. This morning, someone
is singing about getting it right
this time. She puts her coffee in the fridge.
The refrain is dripping from her teeth.
She circles the apartment before leaving,
searching for the answer about the sky
today, what it feels like on exposed skin,
the chance it may open up
into a feverish falling. Somewhere
there, birds are lining into the clouds,
calling into their return. We do this
so often, this rearranging of seasonal
skin, this standing by the front door,
arguing with a stray
glove, a stubborn boot.
Then silence after her departure,
save for heat hissing through the corners.

MOTHER AS GOAT BONE, WRAPPED IN ALUMINUM

Carved out and newly hollow,
I hold you like a coarse tongue
trying not to think of the gossamer cry
stretched out of the velvet of your throat.
Every holiday the same death, a different
small body pinned to the wall,
someone holding a knife, someone holding
your favorite music notes to soothe you,
someone still missed, and you,
a bleached echo of my own hunger,
transitory, a wound clothed
in a faithful hum
to make its worth and weight
some small measurement of holy.

PORTRAIT OF THE COUNTRY IN WHICH I WAS BORN

By now your face is still red and unmanageable. We have peeled it many times,
each time expecting a newer weaving of your complexion, a wreath of an infant

glowing in its casing. Each time we pared away, you howled, teeth
hysterical and flaring in their canals. Before I knew you, I memorized

then translated water into rhythmic chants, blowing a well-tuned hymn
between each ear. We can barely hear anything now over this display,

desperate for memory, I need you to hold still so that we may get this right.
Here is a knife, I will be quicker this time. I will even sing you a song.

BROTHER AS YOUNGER SELF, HUMMING

The streets of Shobra are still traced
with music from years ago—
children ripping
the clothes off lines,
pins scattering in a rounded clatter
of sharp-throated wooden notes.
It may have been a merging
of Mohamed Fouad
and Mohamed Mohie
or Mohamed Fawzi,
and my brother (also a Mohamed)
is sitting in the shimmering corner
of our grandma's balcony with one leg up.
He wants to finish this one song
because it has his favorite parts
which he has rewound a few times now
and Mahmoud is downstairs again
yelling, holding a peeling board game
they taped together and my brother's eyes glint
over to the chorus, remembering how Mahmoud
once told him how his father comes home
only once a month, and he feels bad
he is taking so long to go downstairs
but this would be the last time
he rewinds the song, Mahmoud, *wallahi*,
he yells, the cassette player's volume
on high but not loud enough
to drown out the street market prices,
the chatter of bent men

at the coffeehouse, their fingers caterpillar-like
through the mugs blowing
on clouded tea,
but the music is just enough
to shroud it all in the blur
of a filmy fog that Mahmoud can hear
and he can't help but to remember
how sometimes at night,
if he closes his eyes hard enough,
he hears the din of keys
against the door,
the whistling of a man
nearly always caught
in the middle
of an unfinished song.

THE POULTRY TRADER'S DAUGHTER
INHERITS THE BUSINESS

Tonight, the hens refuse to sleep.
They are sitting in the corner
of the coop, still and wide-eyed.
Even they must know—
an emptying body is still a gift:
rippled, burnt cerise of insides,
the way each pocket of inner skin
folds into the other, esoteric.
Wahashteeny ya omi.
I miss how every dawn,
you'd toss the feed, your hands faithful
to the creatures, to the good work of rising
to the soft beckon of light, to the call of roosters
just as the thinnest nail slit
in the sky is filled with the injury of day.

THE CONDITION, AGAIN

When I talk to my mother about loss
she says human, she says *el rasool*
even the prophet (Peace Be Upon Him)
lost some of his children

and I see him wide-eyed, still searching,
beads between his burning fingers
almost humming ayah after ayah,
his heart newly washed in a tub of snow.

And I am running after him, moss smearing
my shins, yelling out his name
like a fire erupted in my throat, flames
at my teeth curving into a battle.

And he never stops, doesn't turn around,
the cloth he's wrapped within never once
catches on to the branches. His shoulders
spread back to near snapping point.

I hear the nightjar flying from branch
to branch, its call changing each time it turns,
a moth withering on its tongue. Then, later, a stone to throw.

FATHER AS ADOLESCENT, SMOKING

It's early afternoon when you take
to the streets after school.
In this memory, your mother is home
smoothing the creases in your uniform
after sweeping the hen's bloodied feathers
from the kitchen, waiting until you're home
to crush the garlic for the mulukhiyah leaves.
The block not too far from here
always smells of bodies—
the small hamama cooing,
beak breaking from insistent pecking,
rabbits hanging by their hind legs,
skin taut and burning orange,
and your own body, stifled by cotton,
by the ash already starting to spit out
its gray teeth in your lungs,
smoking behind the market again, sun-bent
fingers twitching like dust trying to forget
how your mother was crying
of a dream in which the hand
of every person you ever loved
was reaching for you from a river
whose current surged, their fingers swelling
in the progress, palms barely recognizable,
African tigerfish swarming again and again.
In this memory, you watch the children yell
at each other as the women clip
shirts to the clotheslines, clouded suds
touching your shoes as the butcher across

from you chops a leg, holds it down by its ankle
on the board, saving the feeble bits of wet fat,
pressing between two joints he can't name
but knows how to crack apart in one breath,
the thought of which keeps the cigarette
still between your fingers, suddenly overthinking
the motion, hands hardening at the fact
that any bone can whither, fracturing under
the proper tool and with the right wrist motion
no matter its name. In this memory, you never
put the cigarette out, it hangs from your hand,
insubstantial, as small as the space between
two bones, between two dusty lips left open.

MYTH OF YOUR IMAGINED RETURN

I told you to stop dressing as the savior,
but here you are again at the side of the road,
thin cotton shriveling after the stinging rains
that foggy morning.
You are the heaviest traveler.
You unfold the cloth from your body
and mockingbird feathers fly out of your worn mouth.
Cats gather around at the ends of your bitten shadow,
the potential of insignificant meat, of licks of marrow.
In one palm, a bloodied wing, the raw syrup
of a small existence in the other settling
between the serrated map of your hand,
threads of cloud hanging from your eyelashes.
What else have you halved in this century?

THE PROPHECY

Do you remember July last year in the middle
of the field, warmth hailing from the oak tree,
your face shadowed by the ash pirouetting
from the grave ride suspended above us? You said, *"God,"*
I said, *"Listen for the elk, the lake, the tongue's repetitive laps,*
how often I have said this would hurt us again."
Here is the gift of joy this millennium: the spear torching
through the yew, berries or glass falling, the bull still whole.
You always knew the cows and horses would never make it,
hooves rusting, tied from the birch branches, thorns
between their square dead teeth. After this love,
what's left of our bodies but the eel in our stomachs like ice,
the acid reflux, the lack of control?
I told you what we needed, *told you we would never forget.*

ACKNOWLEDGMENTS

"Brother as Younger Self, Humming," *Poetry*, April 2019

"Myth of your Imagined Return" and "The Prophecy," *Cordella Magazine*

"Father as Adolescent, Smoking" and "The Condition, Again," *Tinderbox Poetry Journal*

"For the Bagged Body in Front of Koshary Ameen Restaurant," *Cordite Poetry Review*, December 2019

GRAY LATITUDES
MICHELLE K. ANGWENYI

Published by Akashic Books
©2020 Michelle K. Angwenyi

ISBN: 978-1-61775-880-5

Akashic Books
Brooklyn, New York, USA
Twitter: @AkashicBooks
Facebook: AkashicBooks
E-mail: info@akashicbooks.com
Website: www.akashicbooks.com

African Poetry Book Fund
Prairie Schooner
University of Nebraska
110 Andrews Hall
Lincoln, Nebraska 68588

TABLE OF CONTENTS

PREFACE
by Patricia Jabbeh Wesley

Michelle K. Angwenyi's *Gray Latitudes* is a body of poems that stretches language to its limit, the subtlety of which surprises the reader as if she wants you to depend on the weight of a word alone. Hers is a rare gift that reminds readers of early Modernist women's attempt to recreate language in ways never done before. There is a Gertrude Stein in Angwenyi's poetics, especially; reading the poems makes you wonder whether what she has said could be possible, and yet you know that, yes, it is possible, because buried deep in each line is the possibility of language.

Perhaps Angwenyi intends to awaken the reader by creating an unexpected space between the poem and the reader; maybe she intends to surprise us, to agitate us with pain and grief. But whatever it is she intends to do, she does so brilliantly by arresting us to a silence that is audible and clear, as in her "Memorial":

> These are the elaborate one-sided goodbyes.
> The learning to accept tea from strangers.
> The voiceless convergence of winds.

> —

> A child half-known,
> their distance half-known

Through brief, tightly woven lines, a mix of prose and free verse, Angwenyi creates new spaces for herself in a world in which many still believe that poetry by Africans or about Africa must explore "traditional" images of Africa. *Gray Latitudes* defies all such norms by navigating the modern literary landscape of the African at home and abroad—a new domain that invites us all to write *our* Africa in its complete modernity and tradition, whatever that is in the new world.

Angwenyi employs in each poem a mournful and meditative voice as her speaker enters into a deep conversation with herself. In the title poem, "Gray Latitudes," the only poem in the collection that mentions her home city of Nairobi, Angwenyi's lament about losses, silences, empty spaces, and longing in a city that "comes and goes" is a shocking reminder that these poems are a daring examination of the realities of a specific place. Even the subtlety of these difficult lines cannot hide the grief in the speaker's voice:

> In this place of colliding times,
> no word for it in childhood, and unrecognizable in this dusk,
> Nairobi comes and goes.
> I had the word for it yesterday,
> and the need that follows, to remember that feeling:
> too-long trousers, newspaper kites, lost boys
> and now, grown-up absences via the labyrinths of other cities.
> There must be a word in which all these lie—
> and through the years-long dust—
> it rises from that airless space on the roof.
> Fills the city with an unnameable grief.

In these poems, Angwenyi paints a picture of the uncertainty of "colliding times," evoking a longing for what was or what is to come. She evokes the fear of not knowing and not having the words to name the painful reality of words that were there yesterday (as in "Nairobi comes and goes") but are no longer there.

Whether she brings us into confrontation with those who "lack the benefit of blood" ("It Is Absurd to Keep the Bones"), or with "A child half-known / their distance half-known," or with "The weight of your hair / and the weight of your sins" ("I Hope You Can Dance Now"), Angwenyi reminds us that: "It is the unfinished silence that carries you, and without asking . . ."

This collection of poems is a powerful testament to the new Africa, which is characterized by the losses that we have inherited, the loss of words even where all around us are words. There is nothing more powerful than the ability to render silence through language, particularly the silence that the unvoiced leave behind when they are no more. Michelle Angwenyi is a new voice among a very powerful group of young African writers, particularly African women poets, emerging into a world that is hungry for such voices from the continent.

MEMORIAL

These are the elaborate one-sided goodbyes.
The learning to accept tea from strangers.
The voiceless convergence of winds.

—

A child half-known,
their distance half-known

—

Escaping the lovers of plants,
tender, soft-hearted, soft-footed,
their lone walks in museums,
the whisperings among fossils.

—

Their dedication to water,
against sound.
The inhabitance of pale yellow.

—

The slowness of arrival. The always arriving.
The day, and its salt pillars.
And the sun, still water.

PART I: GRAY LATITUDES

It is the unfinished silence that carries you, and without asking—after
the earth dug with bare hands, that world-long blue paper with no words,
offered, read wordlessly, in the fragile encounter from a dream—in the last
space in which you could be found, I know this—

(this leftover need to find—)
—there you are:

like skin holding onto scar, still together, but from across this ocean of
indifference. this resistance, this fraud of friction

and at the end of every day, the old man keeps dialing, writing to the light,
inviting it back home, eyes a sadness

like the last word for possibility—

IMAGES

Your images will never leave you. Looking out the window, you will
always see them there. In those moments where a sheet of sentimen-
tality stands between you and what you see, making it both more
and less real. You will turn anything into memory, tired of struggling
to remember. On this Sunday's edge, balancing between the gray of
the trees and the gray of the sky, and just before—an open, empty
yard. In silence, walking as though they are dancing, two women in
white. There is a small fire, and the docility of the broken stone they
walk through and that of the breaking fire they cannot see makes me
believe I have witnessed the modest destruction of a monument—or
its staging. Something about this comes all the way around, from the
small room between a slowly fading imagination and the forthcom-
ing feral apparition to replace it, claiming to protect it, sheltering this
remembrance. And into the Sunday evening, like the knowledge of a
secret, I become aware of it: what's outside the window, in every shap-
ing of its frame, has also been looking in. Monuments: real,
imagined—and all their gray latitudes.

THERE ARE THE FINCHES

Watching birds from the undersides of trees, in a somewhat happy way of
making a clinical void of love. I'm saying that yesterday, I'm pretty sure I
saw a pair of grass finches disappear into the branches, I'm pretty sure I
    know that
[under trees we learn how clouds break.]
I hold this as truth, as a staging away, and to follow: have only been taught
    to love one kind of bird.
So we stay friends in necessity. We stay friends as sky viewed through tes-
    sellating leaves. First thought—I need you to be here with me. Second
    thought: Ah. There are the finches.

PART II: GRAY LATITUDES

In this place of colliding times,
no word for it in childhood, and unrecognizable in this dusk,
Nairobi comes and goes.
I had the word for it yesterday,
and the need that follows, to remember that feeling:
too-long trousers, newspaper kites, lost boys
and now, grown-up absences via the labyrinths of other cities.
There must be a word in which all these lie—
and through the years-long dust—
it rises from that airless space on the roof.
Fills the city with an unnameable grief.
The evenings have never changed wherever you are.
That dread
of being found. But just yesterday,
I learned how to think of the pigeons only, in the sunset,
the ones I would see perched on the orange brick—
and nothing else.
Not even the wooden ones in the house, empty,
not the man they kept company.
But when I remember him, sitting by the ocean, drinking a warm beer,
I only think of the man as one of many men,
still a lost boy—and this is the dust of boyhood:
dancing women of the water, attempts at that washing away,
the evening before you meet God at last, years into your death.

HOW SWIFTLY EVERYTHING FELL INTO PLACE AFTER THAT

It should have worried us that there was no alcohol in the house at the time of his death—that there had been no alcohol for a long time before. We would go and visit, drink in the sun until the curtain had to be closed again, *my eyes are burning*, he said, *apologies*. All he had to offer in those times was tea, no milk. Which we all secretly enjoyed, anyway. It never seemed to grow cold.

It was another one of these days when the lights went off, the day after his birthday. We decided to stay the night, and stuck around for another two or three days, the rice lasting us quite a while. I can't remember who it was who first noticed the glow, who looked at him and saw that his eyes indeed were burning, and demanded to know how he got the fire in there. *I don't know*, he said. *I was just bored, playing alone one night, when it happened.*

After his death, going through his belongings, these are the things we did not know what do with: extensive, detailed catalogues of grief, failures and power outages; a single photograph from the nineties; a weighing scale; a cloudy memory of love; and a porcupine quill with some unknown (unremembered?) initials. We decided to take the quill to the museum; it felt like an artifact they would appreciate.

[These are the bright spots of grief, only ever half of something, half-of-yellow, half of forgetting. This is how one would think of a particular summer, the cast of sliced mangoes, chilli-salt-reddened insides—do you remember the bright weekend figure leaning over the stove, heaving, in and out, heaving: in, and out? and something going wrong in the oven, something else wrong coming in through the window? But outside the kitchen: the sounds of Sunday: children and their footballs, full dresses

12

swaying, Peugeots laughing revived—yet somewhere, barbed wire carved around the shape of top-floor stillness, and carved around something stiller, still: a heaving ceased, something released—released many years ago, in fact, and a summer, Sunday, like today—only beginning to catch up.]

As for what remained, it took us a while to remember the fires, those which were the cause of death. Red, orange, inside his eyes, against the sky. Oh boy. How swiftly everything fell into place after that.

PART I: IN THE SPACE OF WHAT'S ENDED

i hate to think of this delicacy, how to hold things, how to let them trust
you with their skin like glass, like thin glass no ordinary human can make,
should touch, [a trial to not keep asking of you from inside this selfsame
fragility] because

[still, sometimes against everything, you fall into the pavement, impaled
through the air, folded dead, something like atonement

a certain hunger, quenched.]
we, after forgetting, don't have to pretend any more, after desire, with noth-
ing to say

[this is how i write need between, into, separation] and as for the things
that won't leave us alone
(one longs to explain oneself)—

[*i saw that bird on a frozen morning, both, unwrapped forms. and me, we were
both iced on the pavement, for different reasons, but only one of us left that mo-
ment. the other still lives in it, but in the ways
of time at the end of every day, sometimes, it's us both, either dead*

or with nowhere to go.]

PART II: IN THE SPACE OF WHAT'S ENDED

one thing stays the same: lined paper written over on both sides. folded,
and re-folded, falling apart into history. still,
something sutures, holds our life's lines together.
this time, it's different—

you raise the note, broken in four parts, and read it to me. this time,
what i hear is not a story. not even what it's trying to say.
it's what it leaves, half-song, fragments in the room, and from this haunting
there is no ending; every imagined word is washed into your hair, and cut
into the night.
i let the scissors drop, heavy, and there, hands, not yet fallen out of familiarity,
down your back. only later, the unfinishing evening has me looking
into your face, splayed adrift across the years. you speak of code.
(in code.)
as if we had anything left to ask of silence, of touch.

if i had anything to answer to, it might be in the space of what's ended, and
the solitude of these imagined days, days that don't end, shifting from one
end of the world to the other. coming back again.
from this center, we come together once more, unscripted,

everywhere at once, misting through words, asking after each other, as if
in search of suture, only to erase, glide across paper, rewrite— (i speak of
letters, i speak in them)

THE FEAR OF ANIMALS THAT LOOK TOO MUCH LIKE US

Once every night there is the paralysis of not being able to
remember your face; whether laughing wide open or in death
frozen shut [going back to when we were young,
how we don't say we were wrong about it,
when we *are* wrong about it—the animal we saw—]

[it climbs trees these days, it climbs trees in my dreams]

To comfort myself, I say it's changed now, I say it's *changing,*
just not anywhere seen anymore. In its place, there is your ugly old laugh,
and there is my own present face, but even after all this *still* less
the indent of your own.

How to say that.

From this dark blue anger, and all its sunless, twisting animals,
not just given any form, but allowed the choice of their own, too,
we forget to ask why they only ever play with our similarities,
crossing the boundary over and over again, refusing to stay:

And while you are there, not in that space, but *of* it,
how to honor your latitude, how to say that now,
as when we were young, as when we wouldn't have to have
the words, that now, only you don't.

Now, only you are young, and without hands,
only you are growing, climbing a tree somewhere,
perhaps in someone's dream.

ANGER WAS A DARK BLUE

Anger was a dark blue, deepening since
the tedium
of childhood. The evenings, they've
been many, strung through the years. Cracks. Like you say,

irreversible. Now, between places,
something irreversible too, solemn in its transgression, refusal;
as that curl of hair right where your ear bent in.
Familiar not by sight, but by that at-last of love, by that one day you too—

It had always been there. And in your hands, this rot, this
circumstance, this
unavoidable, this eternal—and cease-fire. Transferred. And
this conversation we are both always having, and never got the chance to have.
This hovering, overwhelming I-don't-know.
(But you know.)
And I watched the dark blue blacken, then, disappear.

I HOPE YOU CAN DANCE NOW

Some people are so tender (they are almost like wounds)
(and I hope you aren't hurting) I hope you can dance now.
(I hope you can be touched.)

The weight of your hair
and the weight of your sins, they were once the same,
both the same, but
it is in this space of obliteration that

(Nonetheless—)

I hope you continue to walk in your fields,
and let what was lighter than memory

do what your hands could not.

IT IS ABSURD TO KEEP THE BONES

To be in awe of those that lack the benefit of blood; the benefit of night—
who might still be making use of that still space inside a rose-colored halting.
Now trapped between times, ugly, changeless,
prosecution that continues long after death—
not that we know enough of cameras, but, (and enough with the memorials)—
it is absurd to keep the bones.

SALT

This I know to be sacred—the way you hold salt between your thumb and
forefinger, and the subtle disintegration of what follows after. Sometimes
the sacred is silent, forced into the spaces between letters, utterable in every
word you speak. *Break forth. Lie still. Tilt your head a little to the right.* It's
how you pay attention, those delicate shifts in the spine. It's your eyes that
open with the owls', slanted upwards. Sideways. Weaving colors through
the fossae in music. I know every crevice of your ear—where you hold what
you won't listen to, what twitches when the sound makes its way in—these
made known in my refusal to think of your hands. Except in guessing, in
changing from semitone to semitone; slender noises, shivering through
the walls. In recognition of being—of water, of scent, of spice. Of an ache,
layered in the rust of sunset. In split fruit, this fine lettering, but finer still—
salt between your fingers. And now, mine.

NIGHT-TIME

This time, you have replaced my night-time.
Hands held together become the night-space;
the world sleeps in it. This is the expansion of that first look in the dark,
that sudden sphere of your eyes around us.
This time, we walked down to the blue blur
of lingering between touch, and what precedes it,
stays in between it.
The sticky residue of what-would-have-been
is the deep material of this dream, the freshened air
of Sunday mornings. And the return to the night,
to holding your hair above your head,
and when there is no longer any use for it, cutting it off.
Letting it fall as silent as the suspension of time
when the night is resistant, bloated, cold, insincere,
and someone always leaves for bed too early.

PART III: GRAY LATITUDES

Music fills in, passes through a crack. Arranging
the dance of memory, making you
more aware of it (the crack. Or the music. Or the memory).
One old thing wraps around another. Rightly rendered or not,
it tries to carry you home.
Of those: the soft breaking apart at the end of every day,
an admittance to the lack of language; but along
this continuity, across many days, what makes its way through:
in the elsewhere of gray latitudes, this lack, an abundance.
Songs, made off an odd dependence on death,
on discarded religion, on the remains of dead birds,
all the eternal effluence of remembering
always a dead thing, so in return, within folded tones,
the illusion of a secret that spares your own life
and from it, a whole body of work, and even through the death,
a whole *body*—

ACKNOWLEDGMENTS

"Memorial" appears in *The Mays XXVI* under a different title.

PSALM FOR CHRYSANTHEMUMS
NKATEKO MASINGA

This is a work of fiction. All names, characters, places, and incidents are a product of the author's imagination. Any resemblance to real events or persons, living or dead, is entirely coincidental.

Published by Akashic Books
©2020 Nkateko Masinga

ISBN: 978-1-61775-881-2

Akashic Books
Brooklyn, New York, USA
Twitter: @AkashicBooks
Facebook: AkashicBooks
E-mail: info@akashicbooks.com
Website: www.akashicbooks.com

African Poetry Book Fund
Prairie Schooner
University of Nebraska
110 Andrews Hall
Lincoln, Nebraska 68588

TABLE OF CONTENTS

PREFACE
by Shara McCallum

> Tell the terrain
> that *Iná* is a ghost
> who left her refrain
> in wild animals' throats.

This quatrain from the opening poem in *Psalm for Chrysanthemums*, "Inheritance," establishes the haunted and haunting voice of the speaker in a brief but powerful sequence. The personae of Nkateko Masinga's poems throughout the book are, if not ghosts, then ghostly figures. She is a woman often absent from her own body and life, and the poems act as her attempts to reconcile that feeling with the demands of her relationship to a lover and the role of motherhood, among other things. The speaker's dissociation—the way she holds herself at arm's length, the way she hovers above or outside of herself at times—foregrounds trauma and is the terrain *Psalm for Chrysanthemums* traverses.

After this initial poem, the speaker's existential and psychological condition is alternately revealed and concealed, giving clues that, when pieced together, fashion a story. Altogether, this cycle of intensely lyric poems operates within the register of a fable. The Sylvia Plath epigraph in "For the Ghastly Going" and the three closing poems—"My Lover Pulls Me off the Train Tracks," "My Lover Pulls Me off the Train Tracks, Again," and "My Lover Pulls Me off the Train Tracks Too Late"—speak to a breakdown in the narrator that demands to be read both literally and figuratively. On the top layer, the poems movingly enact the speaker's struggle with mental illness and suicidal ideation. Alongside this seemingly personal narrative, the poems trace another arc: the speaker's attempt to reconcile the love of others with the love of oneself. Ultimately, as with the best of poems, Masinga's spare and unsparing poems raise as many questions as they answer:

4

What is the nature of the self? How does being bound to others—a lover and a child—infringe upon the boundaries of the self? What of who we are must be sacrificed in order to love?

If the poems are allegorical, their lessons are embedded in language that is deceptively clear, and its force becomes apparent often after the fact. Analogously, Masinga's subtle and quick shifts in diction and image, often from the quotidian to the surreal, chisel and propel the poem's tone in many directions at once. Frequently, the tone is unflinchingly honest. Yet the poems are not exactly in the service of confession, or not after truth-telling alone. They carry the urgency to speak, especially of the trauma the female body endures. But as much as the poems present various disclosures, they are equally self-interrogatory. They clarify and hone the "I" through various rhetorical and metaphorical feats.

Recall once more the quatrain I began by quoting. The imperative mood the poet employs in the phrase, "Tell the terrain," makes it seem as if what is about to be requested is straightforward: the speaker has undergone a metamorphosis, transitioning from the living to the dead, and wants now to be seen and heard only as a ghost. But upon closer inspection, the lines are difficult to read as a simple request, one made or one meant to be fulfilled. What would it mean to give up your life in order to plant the refrain of yourself, now transfigured as song, in the throats of wild animals? The poem's masterful use of image and metaphor here, as in many other instances in this and other poems, forces the reader to engage with a paradox: in order to live fully, the speaker of the poem must die. It's no wonder that some of the most memorable lines in this collection encode their contradictory desires in metaphor. What else but images can contain multitudes? Referring to her wish to be released from a world she finds unbearable, the speaker resorts to metaphor as the only way to convey her suffering: "This world is too noisy and tomorrow it will start its engines again."

In Masinga's turn to image, the poems dwell in the realm of archetype and symbol. They are bent on maintaining the centrality of the personal story, while also having that narrative lead to an argument regarding the concept of the self. The poems chart the self's conflicted desires: on the one hand, to connect to those whose bodies hold and offer grounding in this world; on the other hand, to be free of this life and its earthly confines. Masinga artfully constructs a sequence in which death is a strange, troubled path to freedom from the burden of existing for a woman who can only fitfully inhabit herself. The struggle at the heart of the collection is one of the reasons these poems are so piercing and why they remain vital and memorable long after reading them. *Psalm for Chrysanthemums*, whose title prepares us for a song in praise of death, offers a vision that is both beautifully achieved and deeply disquieting.

INHERITANCE

After Audre Lorde

I give birth and my lover renames me
ray of light in Yorùbá. He
says to me:

*"Iná, you have made my world
anew."*

He holds our son
to the sky
and says:

*"Iná, you have illuminated
the darkest of riverbeds
with this gift."*

*"Iná,
our family tree is rooted
in you."*

If the earth spun to my every whim,
I would have stayed with him
to supplement his sun
with new light
each day.

I would have birthed
a lineage,

7

a legion
of brown-bodied
baby boys

who would grow
to host naming ceremonies
in women's wombs.

Instead I grew ill,
my light grew dim,
and his *Iná* was no more.

Light hits water
and reflects,

light hits water
and through our *omi*
I reach for life:

the waves of the sea
are my child's hands
and each morning
I reach for them,

watch him grow,
touch the shore:

my son,
my *omi*.

Each night I disappear

with my lover's light
as the moon stands in
for him, for us.

Before the moon wanes again
we shall come together.

On a night of the full moon,
you can hear the wolves
howl my song:

olówó orí mi
okọ mi

Do you hear the stillness afterwards?
As if the earth wants to know
why *Iná* no longer sings
her own song.

Tell the terrain
that *Iná* is a ghost
who left her refrain
in wild animals' throats.

Everything with breath is an heirloom
Iná left.
Hear her:
in the water, in the air, I loom.

VENUS FLY TRAP

I can count on twelve hands the men I have swallowed whole:
it's a record. If you lined them up, I would be done in a minute

and ask for more. There is no name for what happened to me,
except that men came here and did not return to their homes.

On a Saturday, my doorbell rings and I am sprawled on my bed,
awaiting the inmate whose groans will outmatch my screams.

Amaechi is reported missing on Monday. Do you have a towel
I can use while I watch the news? I join the search party, sated

and confident my belly will not spit him out, feigning a frantic
spell. By noon I am licking my lips. The doorbell rings. *Come in.*

AMAECHI

How carefully we chose our men:
I, Amaechi from the corner store.
You, others. How careful, and yet

I couldn't have been more stupid:

to say *Oluwa* and not mean *God*,
to be begging for a man instead?

Who would have thought I'd tear
so overtly down the middle? *"Say*

a prayer for my love and I: our
revelry has birthed a child, our
child has birthed indifference."

I'm certain this is what it means
to disappear while still alive. *"Sin*
is not magic," Ma said. *"Forbidden*

means just that. He will not return,
save to see if the baby has his eyes."

CATHARSIS

Under our bed,
I find a greying photograph of the woman you loved
and still love on mornings like this,

place it on the mantelpiece for you to inspect,
give you a chance to feign ignorance.

At midday, we separate.

It was inevitable, it seems:

You, having rolled out of the chrysalis of uncertainty
and I, having disentangled myself
from a nightmare that was not mine.

I know now
that the knife the knife-wielder
held against her frame
in my dreams each night
was no common blade.

It was you,
your body,

always so close to her skin,
always so red,
yet I was the one who bled.

FOR THE GHASTLY GOING

"I am not cruel, only truthful."
—Sylvia Plath

I'll take your love in rations: this portion will last till June,
when my leaves turn brown and yours, green. Until June,

when the wind howls in my hemisphere, an overt warning
of the danger to come. Hold the ache in my chest till June,

then tell someone. I am ready to admit this won't last forever:
though I love you dearly, I will only breathe in gasps till June.

I deserved to know there was another love brewing elsewhere.
You are not cruel, only truthful. You may stay here until June,

then pack your heart into your new lover's breast, your ruin
into her decaying chest. Only luck will spare you until June.

PSALM FOR CHRYSANTHEMUMS

The flower of the month was in crisis. At first,
the heading of the article startled me. It said,
"mums are not flowering" and I looked again,
realising I was reading a gardening magazine
with closed chrysanthemum buds displayed.

It was November, the month our love bloomed
and I wished we could give a petal or two away
to the poor chrysanthemums. You laughed, said
I was silly and that I should just pray for rainfall.

I did. I prayed all week, chanted "rain, rain, rain!"
and the chrysanthemums flowered that Saturday.

Rain is another name for love here, I am certain,
because I am in our old garden, kneeling, again.

This time for us, for love to grow in your heart
again. I will chant "love, love, love!" on a night
in mid-February, out of season but just in time
for a few chrysanthemums, and maybe, for us.

REGRESSION

Step 1
When she steals her caregiver's ring
and pawns it
for a fix,
you must say:

*This is not how a testimonial
is supposed to read
for an outpatient,
and her
disinhibition
and inappropriate smiling
are not good signs.*

*Let's book her in
for observation.*

Step 2
When she threatens her mother,
you must say:

*This is not how family feedback
is supposed to read
for an inpatient getting weekend leave,
and her
disinhibition
and inappropriate smiling
are not good signs.*

Let's take away her privileges.
Put her in ward six.

Step 3
When she stabs a nurse,
you must say:

This is not how a progress report
is supposed to read
for a patient wanting to
remain in an open ward,
and her
disinhibition
and inappropriate smiling
are not good signs.

Let's move her to a closed ward.

Step 4
When she develops insomnia
and anxiety,

you must say:

This is why we have drugs:
Serenace
is to
Serenade her

at night.

Disipal
is to make her worries
Disappear
during the day.

Step 5
When a colleague asks:

And the teeth grinding?
The pill-rolling tremor?
The tears?

You must say:

Last resort:
Let's give her Clozapine
or
refer her for pastoral counseling.

Besides,
the prophets said
there would be weeping and gnashing of teeth,
but not like this.

INPATIENT

At the height of my illness, I was (held), detained
(with tenderness, with love), likened to a veld:

In my mania, I was the highveld
with tall plateaus and rolling plains,
too much hill to fit into this world.

In my depression
I was the lowveld,
a failed rift valley
of moodiness
and crying spells.

In the in-between,
the mixed episodes,
the highs and lows
of being part girl-child,
part growing woman

with burnt hands
from every botched attempt
at making a meal,
I was the thornveld:

a semi-arid savanna,
believing I was everything
and nothing
all at once

In the numbness,
the unbearable cold
when I reached for sharp objects
and leaned towards steep inclines

to feel something, anything,

it was erosion that I was compared to:
a sandy beach with all its castles washed away.

In all these states I was (held), restrained.

At nineteen I stumbled
on things that weren't there,

was laughed at for falling,

I shivered when it wasn't cold
and wanted to destroy everything.

Of all the things that I tried to ruin with my hands,
what remained were the bodies of others
(holding) breaking entering tearing into me.

MY LOVER PULLS ME OFF THE TRAIN TRACKS

He holds me, hand against neck, and whispers, *"Thanks for staying"*
into the groove God made for only his fingers, to feel my pulse
and say, *"Oh thank God you're still here. Are you trying to kill me?"*

No, no, darling, only myself.

We drive home in silence, the dogs barking restlessly at the gate,
as if knowing I almost did not make it back.
The sky has readied itself in a coat of grey.
The wind is howling. My lover is sobbing.

I remember spending the Fourth of July in Port Richmond,
lying on a blanket watching the fireworks in wonder.

My host mother asked if the fireworks would trigger me,
if there were wars back home that sounded just like this
and I said, "I came here to forget what home sounds like."

My lover makes Milo with too much sugar, swaddles me
in a black blanket I find more comforting than his arms
and says, "Don't ever do that to me again, you hear?"
I nod, placing my head in his lap.

He knows I will try again. For a moment there is respite, but he
    knows.
This world is too noisy and tomorrow it will start its engines again.

MY LOVER PULLS ME OFF THE TRAIN TRACKS, AGAIN

That night I show him the blade and say,

It does not matter if no train comes.
I am still leaving. Not you, this place.

I am not ungrateful. Your love has trained
me better: I'll make tomorrow's lunch,
our bed, a week's worth of dinners,
love notes you can open on the subway.

My mother taught me to carry an extra ticket
in case I lost one. I sharpen my knife, my spare.

MY LOVER PULLS ME OFF THE TRAIN TRACKS TOO LATE

i

I hover above the body I exited.
He shouts at it, "You wanted this?"
His pain palpable, unlike its pulse.

Its chest one could still percuss—some ciphers of life are deceiving

He stifles the impulse to cuss at
my cowardice (I gave no notice)—some notes aren't worth receiving

What warrants his wrath?
A body is merely a sheath.

I want to say "No. I wanted *us*"—some ghosts are prone to grieving
but I am late, cold. Satan's hiss
and heaven's grip contending.

ii

I abandon the body I existed in—

I follow him, hapless apparition
and suspicious specter-simulate
simultaneously. I meant to stay,
I truly did. Heaven and hell bid
and I chose to return to my love.

I find him with her, happy host
to a lover alive. I, jilted ghost,
hover above my new nemesis—

we brawl for her body. She exits.
I say to my lover, "I wanted *this*."

ACKNOWLEDGMENTS

Thanks are due to the editors of the following publications in which these poems first appeared:

African Writer: "Catharsis"
Green Black Tales: "Amaechi," "Inheritance," "Venous Fly Trap"
Poetry Potion: "Psalm for Chrysanthemums"

THE ORIGIN OF NAME

ADEDAYO ADEYEMI AGARAU

Published by Akashic Books
©2020 Adedayo Adeyemi Agarau

ISBN: 978-1-61775-878-2

Akashic Books
Brooklyn, New York, USA
Twitter: @AkashicBooks
Facebook: AkashicBooks
E-mail: info@akashicbooks.com
Website: www.akashicbooks.com

African Poetry Book Fund
Prairie Schooner
University of Nebraska
110 Andrews Hall
Lincoln, Nebraska 68588

TABLE OF CONTENTS

PREFACE
by Mahtem Shiferraw

The world of Adedayo Adeyemi Agarau's collection, *The Origin of Name*, is filled with ancient knowing: one moment a boy falls out of his mother, new and unrestrained; the next minute he carries "a long line of fathers around his neck" ("Aubade for a Child with His Umbilical Cord Tied around His Neck"). This is what makes Agarau's poetry exceptional—the fact that his words carry with them a long line of ancestors, worlds within worlds— and his careful craft of unpacking these stories produces simple, clear-cut truths. Employing vivid, evocative language, he opens the portals to the otherworlds, sometimes inhabited by benign spirits, or ruthless gods, or the ghosts of his ancestors all blurring at once.

But Agarau's poetry is also inquisitive, at times probing the very essence of the worlds he is exploring. In "First Offering," he writes, "I am a ground, a soil, a field blessed with dead birds . . . I will someday turn into an open city." Here he expresses himself into life (the ground, the soil, the death) and yet represents the nothingness that has defined his life. The poem does not stand in contradiction to itself, and yet it does. Like its speaker, it defies natural definition and instead juxtaposes itself as the originator, a place where the etymology of nothingness, that of invisibility, can be remade as an offering that is a revelation to the reader. Perhaps the collection's greatest strength is that it serves not just as a source of interpretation, but also as a place of comfort. Agarau's speaker is able to exist not just in one world, where the role of fathers and sons blur together but also within multiple worlds. His speaker is shown to be capable of embracing the solitary hybridity that comes from surviving in the liminal space between existences. The speaker claims to be from "a place between earth and heaven, / a sunglass city where each flower plucked is a little child / dying" ("A Child Whose Cry at Birth Suggests Distress").

Agarau is not sentimental in his tone, nor is he self-loathing, and his verses do not express despair. Instead, a distinct sorrow rises just above the surface, a sort of glossed feeling that brushes over the deaths of newborns and children as if they were ordinary occurrences; a sort that refers to men as small gods and to gods as ruthless men. Here, in this collection, is where the poet establishes his distinctive world built by the grief of fathers, the hiding mothers, and so much dying. Agarau describes this world as a place where the soil is rich and the boys come fully formed with the woes of their ancestors, where the knowing and the ancient learning he brings can build an entirely different world, where he can attempt to contain the invisibility of himself and his people and move toward an act of resistance: that of naming things without asking permission, effectively recognizing their existence, their power, and their collective strength.

Agarau's poetry is bold, going where the subjects of the poems themselves haven't gone. The poet chooses to document their lives beyond their understanding. He traces their lineage and their grief back and forth as they cross between worlds. He holds onto their mourning as if it belongs to him. When the invisible war looms large, and the crossing is too much to bear, or comes with too many deaths, it is the poet who takes it upon himself to become the witness to their suffering. He declares himself to be "one who is both flower and a sore" ("The God of Thunder Struck My Father While He Fled the Night I Was Born"), the softness, the beauty, and the light contained in his earthbound body.

By defying the unspoken decree of the gods, Agarau's poetry shifts the focus of the crossings from the worlds to the subjects themselves, carrying the readers along with him as his cowitnesses, recognizing that the collective suffering of the subjects/characters that people these poems is too much to bear, especially as they continue to experience so much dying around them. By bearing witness to their grief, the poet establishes himself as a mediator of sorts—one that stands between the gods, the spirit world, and the earthbound—serving, in a sense, as the alternative subject to carry their collective mourning. Agarau's poems instruct and dictate the way we come to understand the intricate interconnectivity and fluidity of such worlds. His speaker provides a radically new space to inhabit, even as he knows himself to be one that was also fed with "a god's leftover." He dreams of becoming a god so he can rearrange history, offering this gathering of poems as a safe passage, one filled with wonder, crossing and containing, and so much light.

Agarau's debut collection is truly an exceptional one. He labors to ensure that his craft and language are suitable conveyors of the intricacies and complexities of Yoruba thought. His unapologetic tone is tempered by moments of disarming softness even as he renames his people over and over again in what amounts to an act of both resistance and kindness.

AUBADE FOR A CHILD WITH HIS UMBILICAL CORD TIED AROUND HIS NECK

the ferocity of that rain   announced your coming   called
you a door with a broken knob   we know what a shadow turns to
when mixed with light   your mother dreamed that a ship wrecked
in her stomach   and she howled a storm back into her mouth

the gods stilled the room from the corner where she sat
salt & bone fell into the same plate   a long-dead ancestor twisted in his
home of sand
            a boy falls out of his mother carrying
            a long line of fathers around his neck

ORUNMILA

Sea was named sea when a village gathered to watch a man emerge from salt. A palm dove sat on his shoulder. Orunmila opened his mouth & we saw a convention of butterflies. We saw wings & trees, a forest of wild angels beckoning to us. The first miracle he did was to teach us how to name things. We named sea. Named each bird according to their songs. Named each god according to what they eat.

FIRST OFFERING

The priest and my mother's faith are tender flowers.
I am a ground, a soil, a field blessed with dead birds.
I am a sinister wind in the east of this place.
My mother will rise to the empty window
and bless the road.
Everything nameless is as empty as a jar filled with silence,
as empty as the void upon the sea
on Sundays. I am seashells and coral,
wild winds brushing the bruises of its own knees.
My mother will fasten me into a prayer,
fasten me into the anguish boiling in her chest.
I am an empty room, a word in my ear
is as loud as the velocity of receding echoes.
I will someday turn into an open city
—a boy who finally knows that he is lost,
that he is this close to his grave,
or his grave is as empty as his mouth.
I will someday turn into a vase full of flowers.

But my mother says that the gods are waiting by the door.

HOW WE BURY A CHILD THAT DIDN'T MAKE IT HOME ALIVE

They say to the mother, *do*
not come out before the sun

because that is where
the father nurses his grief.

A boy fetches the spade and each time
a spadeful of sand is dug. The father

turns into a leaf.

A bit of him falls slowly
into the palms of the gods

A red napkin tied around his waist,
the man says prayer into the soil

blessing the gods that give
the sun but take a son.

AN ANALYSIS OF ISOLATION
AFTER KIRIJI WAR

As the cannon hit the rock beside a hut where a mother nursed her son, their bodies were smothered into a puree of blood & bones. Warriors ran against winds, their mouths pushing incantations against rivers, against time. Drums rose to the ear like storms. A little boy stood amidst the chaos, crying, searching the earth full of dead bodies for his *ma'ami*. The sky ferried fireballs into Ibadan.

We must not forget that we once sang in the innocence of children before
    we grew up greet
white bodies on our shores, before they asked us *who amongst you is the*
    strongest?

A PORTRAIT OF MY SISTER AS TALABI

In her mind, she is freshly baked bean
from a kitchen of echoes where mothers
name their girls after hurricanes and storms,
a room blessed with ghost and mothers' mothers,
each journey a blessing of palms. My sister
is not a palm frond, she is a tree blown in wind.
She does not dance to the whistle of her father's
blessing. My sister stands before a mirror,
counts the number of eyes growing on her skin.
She bows her head in prayer & returns to the grave.

A CHILD WHOSE CRY AT BIRTH SUGGESTS DISTRESS

I say I come from a city where we wash our wounds with salt,
where we give every sore a new name just so they feel new;
a place where god sits between sun & waterfalls,
angels lifting lanterns against darkness.

I am from a place between earth and heaven,
a sunglass city where each flower plucked is a little child
dying. We exalt names over people; crunch their bones
and hold our screams behind our lips.

THE GODS ASK US TO MAKE AN OASIS

They call us little gods
     because we fall too often like rain,
because we are named after storms,
     because our bodies are made from clay
breakable like lightning,
     breakable like promises.
The gods gave us tongues
     to call every darkness in us
by its names, by the fire in its eyes.

The gods ask us to bring salt and sprinkle it on this soil,
     to beckon earth mothers to rise from flames,
to give us dreams wide enough to ferry us,
     to build us a boat and name each land a city across the sea,
give us feathers and wings and letters and names.

BANTALE DROWNING IN A FLOWER ROOM

Perhaps this is how you love to be seen:
a shaved head, with a mother crying
into a bowl; a lamp blown by
raging wind; a father's silence as he
watches *baba* chant into your ears.

Perhaps you love your body burst
dead and growing from butterfly back
to moth.

Perhaps it is your joy that, in
this room, silence is what carries us.
A father shuts his eyes against his tears,
calls your name silently, but the gods have taken
your body.

Perhaps your name wasn't yours.
Bantale is *stay with me till dying age.*
It is also your mother calling you out of *iroko*
to unmake every journey you have made.

Perhaps each of your exiles
is a reminder that home
is the paradise of woods.

THE NAMING OF THINGS

An elderly man once sat on a wooden chair beside his mud house,
told stories of how gods rode the back of clouds till they found
a preservation of bodies. He told stories of how oduduwa
plucked the sun like a fruit from the sky & gave it to moremi;
how a mother once became oil and water all at once. He told of how
the earth was once flat and how he walked to the gateway
into heaven at olumirin. How warlords became rocks at idanre,
a safehouse for children and mothers when war returned.
Afterwards, our fathers named everything falling into and
out of the sky after a god.

ABIKU

Imagine this child as a god bending shadows in water.
Imagine it as a room full of doors, a mother walking

through a forest of penance and flagellation. Imagine
that this child is heavy because it is full of goings.

Imagine each closed door is a mother
crying her child back into her womb.

Imagine the grave as a reunion
of kids falling out of their mothers' wombs.

Imagine a tree full of birds fallen,
from a tree, from a mother, each thud aching.

Imagine them switching their mothers'
lullabies into dirges.

THE GOD OF THUNDER STRUCK MY FATHER WHILE HE FLED THE NIGHT I WAS BORN

So the elders gathered to ask themselves,
what shall we name this one who is both flower and a sore?

So they collected my father's body and burnt it,
fed his ashes to the god of thunder and fed me
with a god's leftover.

I still dream of clouds opening each time I think of leaving.

IN THIS POEM THE GOD OF IRON TAKES OVER A CHILD

Ogun sees a dog instead of a child,
a spitting cobra instead of a girl.

It sees blood in place of mother's water breaking,
sees a blade in place of a palm. Ogun hears distant barking,

so it runs into the house where a new child is born
to take over its body. We hear howling instead of cries.
A flower bleeding from its stigma.

Ogun's body is made of machetes, so it cuts this child
the way a knife cuts a dog, cuts his mother and
plucks every laughter from this house.

[A QUESTION ABOUT LOSS]

How shadow
becomes an
empty house
is god's work.

You can't tell me
the earth was not
made with appetite.

You can't say
art is why the ground
opened to swallow
your father's body.

We have come
in tears
measuring ashes
into a flower vase

where we solemnly fit
his body.
           He is deserted
like a forsaken Christ.

The cleric says we were made to leave,
to elope without the body.

The cleric says only the gods
know when.

I ask why he doesn't let us
say goodbye.

THE CROSS AND THE CROSSING

Before the crossdressers come to nurse my wounds
I revolt. I beckon the shadows of Orunmila,
the half-sized god of salt whose son
knew when the earth was just a seed.
At the end where the story turns into a blood feast,
when the ground opens because a boy has fallen,
when the sun crawls into the back of his palms,
the shadow emerges from water.
There is nothing as pungent as a crucified baby
His last sound comes as language twisted
between bruised tongues. The boy begs to be free,
begs to be a seed at the feet of a tree.
The cross & the crossing, The cross & the crossing.
The doors are unlocking: ephrata.

NOTES ON
RESILIENCE
SAFIA JAMA

This is a work of fiction. All names, characters, places, and incidents are a product of the author's imagination. Any resemblance to real events or persons, living or dead, is entirely coincidental.

Published by Akashic Books
©2020 Safia Jama

ISBN: 978-1-61775-886-7

Akashic Books
Brooklyn, New York, USA
Twitter: @AkashicBooks
Facebook: AkashicBooks
E-mail: info@akashicbooks.com
Website: www.akashicbooks.com

African Poetry Book Fund
Prairie Schooner
University of Nebraska
110 Andrews Hall
Lincoln, Nebraska 68588

TABLE OF CONTENTS

PREFACE
by Hope Wabuke

Safia Jama, a Somali and Irish American poet who grew up in New York City, is a daughter of the diaspora. Her collection, *Notes on Resilience,* is divided into two sections: "Part I: Somalia" and "Part II: Home Leave." The poems reckon with the nature of home and the shifting of identity in the movement between cultures and countries.

The examination of home permeates the text, from the organization of the book, to the titles of poems, and to the content of the poems themselves. Haunted equally by her father's Somali homeland and by his absence when he travels alone for work to Somalia, the speaker in these poems brings together fragments of memories to form a coherent, complete puzzle of selfhood. "*How is the family back home?*" asks the narrator in the opening poem, "Dad's Last Visit," only to be met with:

> Dad's voice drops to a lower
> register—harder to hear.
>
> I fix my eyes
> on the alligators
> still circling the moat.

The threat of violence, here characterized by the hungry-toothed animals and the watery barrier, is potent. Combined with the rapid scansion created by the short lines, this imagery evokes a sense of the uneasy tension present in both characters' relationships to home. What is revealed here is a complication: the gothic underbelly portending that all is not as well as it would appear on the surface.

Jama's chosen milieu is the quiet moments of the everyday: she shows us a gift being given, the making of a cake, awful television. These are the

moments that are often overlooked because it may not seem world chang-
ing. However, because of the depth of Jama's observations and lyric inten-
sity, these moments are embedded with larger resonance, proving a deft
ability to evoke the profound with the seemingly mundane. In "My White
Mother Makes Lemon Meringue" Jama writes:

> Mother makes   lemon meringue
> separating yolk   from egg white
>
> the way ocean   religion   melanin
> keep me   from my kin.

Here, the act of separating the parts of the egg that is a basic element
of baking becomes imbued with the meaning of the separation of the two
parts of the speaker's self: the Somali and the Irish American. The tension
the speaker feels between these two parts of her ethnic heritage becomes
resonant through the use of imagery, thus becoming immensely relatable
and universal. A compelling layer here is that, to make the prized end result
of lemon meringue, the egg whites and colored yolk are segregated into two
spaces, the meringue "topping" and the filling—in a telling comment about
how the speaker feels her identity is engaged within this space, an ocean
away from the "religion" and "melanin" of her kin.

Jama's poems engage in a critique of gender norms through the ex-
ploration of her complex relationships with the men in her life. Home is
still the milieu, yet the ideas are expansive in their implications. The idea
that she must defer to her brother's desires because he is male allows her
to explore the unsettling fact that she must defer both to the patriarchy—
and the patriarchy's obliviousness to its privilege—and to its penchant for
meaningless destruction.

Masculinity, especially in relation to family, is an idea that Jama looks
at in great depth in this collection. In her poem "My Brother's Menagerie,"

she writes:

> I keep a menagerie
> of beasts my brother set free
> then set upon me.
>
> He kept a tin of cookies
> under the bed.
>
> I went to him:
> I needed
> his daily feedings.
>
> Today all the empty cages
> in my head wait
> for the wildest memory.
>
> Animals may hurt
> each other in captivity—
>
> but a baby elephant
> left alone
> will surely die.

Here, in the merging of the fantastic and the real to critique patriarchal gender roles reflected in the family, Jama reveals an imagination reminiscent of Natalie Diaz.

If the first half of the collection is haunted by the father's absence because of travel, the second half of the poetry collection is haunted by the father's absence through death. This sentiment is most potent in the title poem, "Notes on Resilience," opening thusly: "Mom writes *Dad is fading*."

The poem continues on to reckon with death as a lasting absence before closing with the raw intensity of these lines: "What is it to lose a father? / How can a mountain disappear?" It is almost as if the speaker is surprised that the father's death should rhyme so harshly, even with his prior absences. Because of the finality of his death, the speaker understands that, "what is not there / can no longer touch you, / whether to harm or hold."

Resilience, says Jama, is to create value and meaning where it has been denied. To mourn, understand, and move forward. Because we must.

I
SOMALIA

DAD'S LAST VISIT

I'm in my midthirties,
but I still drag my Fisher-Price
toy castle to the center
of the area rug.

My niece, I see,
has been playing.

I find a plush raccoon
behind the drawbridge,
a doll wedged in the tower.

Indignant, I mess up her system.

Put the raccoon in the tower,
hide the girl doll.

I examine a souvenir-sized
Somali flag, blue with a white star,
which someone has pinned
to the spring pole
with a pink barrette.

Dad jokes,
If the president of Somaliland saw that, I'd be fired.

Silently, I hope he does get fired.
I miss him.

Little do I know, he'll soon be
home for good.

The doctor in Nairobi will say,
quit fooling around.

Dad will return to Burao
for one last goodbye,
then come home to us
and the world's best hospitals.

I don't know this as I inspect
my old toy castle,
rescued from the trash
by my mother.

That castle became my signature toy.
Safia's Castle. Indestructible.

I press open the trap door
and see the prisoners have had
a little hay to sleep on
all these years.

My castle gives me the courage to ask,

How is the family back home?

Dad's voice drops to a lower
register—harder to hear.

I fix my eyes
on the alligators
still circling the moat.

TWO GIFTS

I got a carousel
of carved horses:
pastel pinks, blues, greens,
safely the most beautiful toy
our garden apartment had ever seen.

And Grandma Shine gave my brother
a flashlight that resembled
a roll of Life Savers.

And he was quiet a moment
before he began to whisper
about the beauty of his
Life Savers flashlight, all bright
red yellow green with possibility of light
and hope of rescue
from the dark
where I spent my days
playing alone
in a closet upstairs.

How long did it take?
Five minutes? An hour?

I gave him the carousel,
I consented.
He didn't have to pry
it from my fingers.

My brother had a way
of getting his way:
twice my size,
twice my age.

His powers were godlike,
omniscient.

Not my mother
not my father could stop him
after he ran out of tears.

I went off to play with my flashlight,
I didn't mind too much.

I didn't see him fish
the toolbox out from under the bed.

He used a screwdriver
to loosen the horses
from their stable.

Not stable,
more like a little stage
where they pranced
to a tinkling melody
that came from a golden wand
shaped like a butterfly.

What he had done.
What he had undone.

The glittering bones
of the music box,
splayed open.

A few horses, half-broken
on the carpet.

Grandma woke from her sleep
in the next room.
Her heart was weak
and her face turned to stone
as she said my brother's name
like a curse.

He just wanted to see how it worked.
And besides that,
I had given it to him,
he kept saying.

She gave it to me
She gave it to me

Yes, I had been given a gift
of music and song and horses
and he had been given—what?
A flashlight? We didn't live
in the country and hadn't had
a blackout since '77.

I couldn't have been much older than seven
the day my brother took me apart

with tools
from the family toolbox.

He lined up the instruments on the blanket.
I lay still under the ether.

He nodded to me each time
like a surgeon
nodding to his nurse.

Sometimes grace is a child,
looking away.

I didn't see
what he had done,
what he had undone.

The glittering bones
of the music box
splayed open.

A few horses, half-broken
on the carpet.

And those that remained
seemed now chained there.

I looked away from all that,

the closet door
ajar.

THE VICTORIAN ERA

It was a long period of peace, prosperity, refined sensibilities and national self-confidence. And crumpets.

The Whigs became the Liberals.
With strawberry jam.

Pax Britannica. Economic, colonial and industrial consolidation, temporarily disrupted by the Crimean War in 1853.

Quiet please, this is a library.

The end of the period saw the Boer War and a widening voting franchise. Beware of the wild boar roaming the library!

Lord Melbourne, Benjamin Disraeli, Lord Salisbury a.k.a. Most Honorable:

". . . a patient, pragmatic practitioner, with a keen understanding of Britain's . . . interests. He oversaw the partition of Africa."

You're a *good* patient, my dear.

Sir Robert Peel, Lord Derby, and Lord Palmerston. William Ewart Gladstone. We're so *glad* to see you.

Ireland's population, however, decreased sharply.

Good night, Irene.
Good night.

MY BROTHER'S MENAGERIE

Little elephants behind the trees
don't want to be found.

A few still live in the forest.

The only way to find them
is to befriend (or pay) a local.

I pay a therapist each week.

The days I break,
she gives me sea glass,
bits of coral.

I keep a menagerie
of beasts my brother set free
then set upon me.

He kept a tin of cookies
under the bed.

I went to him:
I needed
his daily feedings.

Today all the empty cages
in my head wait
for the wildest memory.

Animals may hurt
each other in captivity—

but a baby elephant
left alone
will surely die.

AGNES MARTIN RETROSPECTIVE

After the show at the Guggenheim, I decide that I am a walking
Agnes Martin painting.

Not unlike walking pneumonia, I walk around with this condition,
just as, passing through the halls of the museum, I wear a faded grey
coat that somehow evokes the surface of her canvas.

People stare in disbelief, back and forth, between me
and the paintings, unable to distinguish the two of us.

Like the Agnes Martin, I have sharp lines
that blur and we both feel a sense of vertigo looking down.

Later in life, I am black and blacker, much like the black pyramids
that appear in her otherwise European geospace territories.

Like an Agnes Martin, people think of me as calm and serene
while inside, I rail and rage.

So I make my sharp angles more and more soft
like a kid's new eraser.

I want to clothe myself constantly in Agnes Martins,
and always be that safe and serene

and carry little cards that say
"Untitled."

BREAM

The fish twists its way
across my plate,
    a cold eye cast open.

I like the sound,
    Bream.

How it rhymes
    with *glean* and *dream.*

So I lift a bonsai tree
    of bone,
loosen a morsel
    of brined flesh:
I taste this new
    word.

I've eaten
oceans of bream
    as a child.

LIES

Besides a lie / I own nothing.
　　　　—Liu Xiaobo

Cloud was the name of my gray horse.
I collect dollhouses.

I stand to inherit an igloo and my mother's old polar bear collection.
I harbor all the melting ice caps in my mouth.

Sea lions hide from the polar bears in my cavities.
My baby teeth grew in white gold, which is to say yellow.

I am a sculptor at heart.
I'm big in Singapore.

In the third grade I sculpted a life-sized woolly mammoth out of melted down
wedding bands.

These days, I make swans from tinfoil that once wrapped the cheese sandwiches
Mother made.

I never loved you.

All the polar bears are crying because you are so beautiful and warm,
they say it's killing them.

The seals are synchronized swimming again, like sad old ladies
in frilly bathing caps.

My grandma nicknamed me Lemonade because I was yellow and ridged and buttery as popcorn in that yellow sweater.

Twelve years of ballet.

And my pet sea lion lived to be one hundred and seven.
She never, ever died.

No one ever dies.

II
HOME LEAVE

TWO SISTERS

I.

I was nineteen when my father
took my picture somewhere near
the Somali-Ethiopian border.

I stood frowning in a flowing dress,
red fabric loosely covering my hair.

Dad blinked in disbelief, calling me
Ghost, apparition risen out of the dust.

*

He tells me about his sisters
ten years later,
one airless summer
when time hangs heavy
around my neck
and I think *I could get
pregnant to fill the silence.*

Instead, I mutter something
about an Oral History.

II.

We sit at the dining table—
my father, delicate postsurgery,
and perhaps a little hurt
that I married while he was away
on one of his endless
humanitarian missions.

Now he is too afraid of death
to touch another cigarette,
so he can't slip outside
to smoke and dream.

I ask about our Somali family,
unknown to me except for the faces
of kin whose names I quickly forget.

I serve a pasta primavera
and then ask,

What about your sisters?
You never talk about them

My sisters?

He clinks the sides
of the mug with a spoon
and travels back fifty years.

III.

One day a man,
grey-haired, respectable,
arrived to court my eldest sister
who practically had raised me,
with Mother being so busy.

Our family had to drop everything
to entertain the suitor and his family.

The sight of all that food—
the slaughtered goat and kid,
camel's milk, ghee, rice,
and all the rest
all turned my stomach.
I could barely eat a thing!

Finally, on the fifth day
Sister gave her consent.

Did she have a choice?

Yes, yes, she could have refused him,
but they married.

[He pauses, hums very softly]

Six months later, she died of cholera.

Nomadic tradition dictates
that a bride's early death
is a debt to be paid.

My sister Arfi was nearly thirteen.
A shy, pretty girl.

Now the eldest daughter.

IV.

My father was teaching second
grade at a British boarding
school in the cool mountains
of Somaliland when he
received the rare telegram:

*Your sister Arfi died
giving birth to her third child*

Where to put this fact
amid math and English lessons,
and scenes from the Arabic
romance novels he read
most afternoons?

Once, he tried to read
Austen's *Pride and Prejudice,*
but it was a stone, impenetrable
to the child of Somali nomads,
with its premise of universal
truths about marriage.

V.

I'm thinking of the Child ballad,
"Two Sisters."

The miller, who makes a fiddle
from the younger sister's bones.

What did he doe with her fingers so small?
He made him peggs to his violl withal

*

Grandma's womb must
have clenched
with double-grief.

Another daughter lost:
given to that gentleman caller.

His camel caravan bound for eternity.

MY WHITE MOTHER MAKES LEMON MERINGUE

Mother makes   lemon meringue
separating yolk   from egg white

the way ocean religion melanin
keep me   from my kin.

Hands strain   my Somali cousins
into the half-broke shell: a failed state.

Mother labors for hours   mashing cold butter
into flour dropping ice water   onto dough.

I labor too—
trying not to   puncture the yellow center

so as not to muddy   what's clear
or say   what's muddled.

As the meringue's stiff peaks rise,
I swallow words like the *has*

in chasm—   chew silence
lose   the taste of my   foreign tongue.

I lick the bowl *clean.*

NOTES ON RESILIENCE

Mom writes *Dad is fading.*

And that is fitting,
for tonight's moon is leveled
into a perfect half.

Peace is not so much a presence
as an absence—
what is not there
can no longer touch you,
whether to harm or hold.

You're through and so full of wind
even the leaves have left.

A student of mine once said
Father is like mountain.

I didn't understand.

She said *Father* again
and again in her language
but I couldn't produce the sounds.

What is it to lose a father?
How can a mountain disappear?

PUBLIC TELEVISION

As my father lay dying, what seemed cruelest that night
was that, truly, there was nothing good on TV.

We watched Hari Sreenivasan roam around Central Park,
looking for Pokémon, obviously bored and questioning

whether he had taken a wrong turn in his career, and soon
my father was nodding off, and I felt indignant that we couldn't

at least provide him with some form of meaningful, if light,
entertainment for his penultimate month on earth;

my father had been a passionate watcher of the nightly news,
and I knew, in his final weeks, that the news had let him

down like a bad old friend, and there was nothing decent
to watch, nothing with heart or substance that could make

my father cry like in the old days, watching a tawdry
television movie on Lifetime with Mom asleep on the love

seat, and me awake as he raised a hand to his face and said,
"Don't tell anyone I cried," and I would nod slowly

because I had already started tailgating during the commercials,
but listen, who is to blame here and when exactly did it happen?

I still think we have a choice here, but I don't fault my father
for turning away from the world and from our television set—

once, he tossed our wood-paneled, black and white boob tube
in the trash, raging like a maniac after my brother wouldn't turn

the damn thing off, and Dad blew up—we woke up the next day

and had a color TV, and my brother slid off the hook like an old
sturgeon, too ugly to eat and almost admirable in his set ways

and, no, I couldn't blame my father for dying because I understood
that this world was no longer for him,

there was nothing good on, and he showed great courage
as the screen went dark.

HOME LEAVE

A girl walks out the door and into the half-yellow light.
Why did the chicken cross the road? and other questions
riddle her mind. Piss trickles down her leg: she lets it.
She crosses a black river to reach the playground.
She crosses a black river in her mind.
Where are you going, little girl?

Sometimes I feel like a motherless child,
a long, long way from home.

Memory: my father placing shirts into a light blue suitcase.
Mother, annoyed. *You always leave it till the last minute.*
I'm the same way. I sniff around the suitcase, tentatively.
I drag it out, then think, why not pack light? A bundle
tied to the end of a stick would do just fine.
1983. My father is flying to Ethiopia.
You can't go, I say. There is no food. You'll starve.
Don't worry, he laughs. I will have plenty of food.

Sometimes I feel like a motherless child,
a long, long way from home.

My mother will find me alone in the empty playground.
She will tell me the story, years later, wrist dangling over the
     steering wheel.
You were so little, she will say. Too little to be left alone.
Ruth, you see, needed my help. She begged and begged.
My mother will wipe away a single tear. I will walk to the empty
playground. I will wait in her nightmares, sitting on a swing.

Sometimes I feel like a motherless child,
a long, long way from home.

ELEGY

We watched other families and choked on the smoke from strange grills.

We drank whiskey in the dry heat and planted trees without names.

We thought we saw an oasis in a clock tower but that was a movie.

We crocheted little children.

We heard the school bus groan on the long ride home.

We pitied the unhappy couples shipwrecked in restaurant windows.

We defended the old baseball stadiums and coveted other people's dogs.

They did not belong to us, but we still missed them.

NOTES

"Two Sisters" quotes from "The Twa Sisters" found in *English and Scottish Popular Ballads*: Student's Cambridge Edition. Ed. Helen Childe Sargent and George Lyman Kittredge. 1904.

"The Victorian Era" utilizes information and language from the Wikipedia page of the same title, accessed on July 31, 2015. The poem ends with a fragment from Leadbelly's "Irene Goodnight."

The epigraph for "Lies" is from Liu Xiaobo's poem, "Experiencing Death" excerpted in "Words a Cell Can't Hold," *New York Times*. Opinion, December 8, 2010.

"Home Leave" quotes the refrain from "Motherless Child," an American Negro spiritual. This particular phrasing comes from an interpretation by the folksinger Odetta.

ACKNOWLEDGMENTS

"Two Gifts": *Ploughshares*
"Agnes Martin Retrospective," "The Victorian Era": *BOMB Magazine*
"My Brother's Menagerie": *Wildness*
"Lies": *Boston Review*
"My White Mother Makes Lemon Meringue": *Cave Canem Anthology XIII*
"Elegy": *Muftah*

The author would like to gratefully acknowledge a few of the people who made this work possible.

Thank you to my teachers: Rigoberto González, Brenda Shaughnessy, Rachel Hadas, A. Van Jordan, Cynthia Cruz, Tyehimba Jess, and Hettie Jones. Thank you to Cave Canem, especially to Cornelius Eady, Toi Derricotte, and Alison Meyers. Thank you to Jayne Anne Phillips, Melissa Hartland, and my colleagues from the Rutgers University–Newark MFA program.

Thank you to the people who gave me invaluable feedback and reliable support along the way: Helen Morrissey Rizzuto, Alison Roh Park, Cynthia Manick, Leila Ortiz, Vincent Cross, Anisa Rahim, Anthony Cirilo, Andrés Cerpa, Matthea Harvey, J.P. Howard, Lynn Melnick, Naomi Extra, Gail Noppe-Brandon, and Anna Holtzman.

Thank you to Kwame Dawes, Chris Abani, and Ashley Strosnider. Thank you to Johnny Temple and Akashic Books.

Thank you, Hope Wabuke.

Finally, thank you to my family. I love you.

YELLOWLINE
FATIMA CAMARA

Published by Akashic Books
©2020 Fatima Camara

ISBN: 978-1-61775-882-9

Akashic Books
Brooklyn, New York, USA
Twitter: @AkashicBooks
Facebook: AkashicBooks
E-mail: info@akashicbooks.com
Website: www.akashicbooks.com

African Poetry Book Fund
Prairie Schooner
University of Nebraska
110 Andrews Hall
Lincoln, Nebraska 68588

TABLE OF CONTENTS

PREFACE
by Honoree Fanone Jeffers

Women collect blood through memory, and memory begins with particular truths. Memory changes. It morphs as each line of blood runs through a family and crosses with new lines. As women push their progeny into life, that life springs into descendancy. As I read *Yellow*Line by Fatima Camara, I was struck by the way she fashions women in verse—her grandmother, her mother, herself—and how these women intersect.

*Yellow*Line begins with "Forward," a poem about a beloved grandmother who now resides with her ancestors. Separated into sections, this is a narrative presented in beats: the birth of the speaker's mother, the passing of the speaker's grandmother, and finally, the burial of the speaker's grandmother, when "the dirt became / a new home." The grandmother's interment is not viewed as an end, however, but as merely a relocation, implying that life goes on after death. A different domestic locale will welcome this grandmother; perhaps it is a place with a kitchen and a bedroom with a soft, sheet-covered mattress.

The memory of the speaker's grandmother is strong—pulsing—in her daughter, and it is implied in the granddaughter who witnesses her own mother's transformation. The grandmother's child is taken over by grief and a spiritual longing. She prays to join her lost kin in the afterlife:

> five times a day,
> wet with ablution,
> begging God to bring her
> closer to the sky.

Readers aren't sure if, as the speaker's mother did, the grandmother also crossed the sea from Gambia to America, or if the grandmother remained in West Africa and died there. We only know that the grand-

4

mother, the matrilineal marker of the family, is no longer alive in body but occupies a space in her daughter's spirit.

Camara continues to explore themes of maternity in "Of Breath," a poem about the speaker's first encounter with water within the artificial boundaries of a pool. The language of this poem approaches spare, but one can almost smell the chlorinated water in which the speaker longs to play. Yet something frightening lurks in this water, because the speaker's mother avoids the pool:

> my mother's fear of going
> under has everything
> to do with breath
> the fear of
> losing it.

The recurrence of this mother figure throughout the chapbook allows the reader to carry over emotional information from one poem to the next. Thus, *this* mother's fear of water may be logically primal—the threat of drowning—or it may be that she does not want to be reminded of crossing another body of water and the separation from her own maternal source, as happened in the earlier poem. Later on, a rapid turn informs us this mother's fear may be learned because of domestic strife:

> still
> the summer
> we forgot our dad,
> there was a day
>
> she went in the water,

The phrase "forgot our dad" *muddies* this water, for one might wonder:

was this father forgotten, or was he discarded? Now, we live in a space where the most important figure of this poem is a remaining woman, one who enters the water alone. Water is the symbol of motherhood, and the mother is submerged in symbolism; thus, motherhood truly rules this poet's verse.

Camara's use of volta that plays out through quick, imagistic gestures highlights her subjective profundity. Though every poem in this collection is focused on narrative, the application of volta creates movement that readers of contemporary American poetry have come to expect from predominantly lyric poems. Even without Camara's narrative stories, these suddenly slanted meanings elicit reader curiosity. "Anew" starts out as a love poem—and again, through spare implication, a woman-centered poem—but one small pronoun marks this entire narrative with trauma: "It hurt every time, how I said yes to survive." What is "it"? Sex? Love? Or simply the affirmative utterance of "yes"? We're never really provided an answer, and while we attempt to further interrogate, the poem abruptly ends: "Besides, he tried to make a ghost of me first." With volta, Camara offers memorable tenacity. While a strictly lyric poem might not have staying power, what is *not* said in this poem urges the reader to return, to look at clues that are wrapped in figurative language, and to remember.

Camara ends this collection in the profound way that she began, with ancestry: a woman who has borne a female line, a woman mourned even after death, a woman for whom her descendants long. In "Erosion," again, a clearly stated narrative purpose: "I miss my grandmother." This longing is enrobed in language that both adheres to and diverges from narrative. Here, as elsewhere, Camara's language is accessible, which is important to the arc of her collection. She does not attempt to confuse the reader; connection is her purpose—and acknowledgment.

FORWARD

i.
grandma
never spoke of her mother.

and couldn't believe
when in front of her
came a girl
calling out *mom*
to whom she gave birth.

couldn't believe
she had become
greater than what she lost

so long ago.

ii.
when the dirt became
a new home
for grandma
mom began to pray more.

five times a day,
wet with ablution,
begging God to bring her
closer to the sky.

uncle argues
that death is not

what brings a person to God.

sure.

but grandma's absence
keeps mom's lips
to the floor.

iii.
there must be no language left
after you've lost who
gave you yours.
tongue dry with grief.

there must be a burial ground
for all the lost words.
a world where the tongue can
mirror the woes
and all the orphaned children
are not desolate in their speech

iv.
I have plenty of memories
with grandma. some I would
never share with mom,

some that are fading,
some mom was there for,
and all, she refuses to speak about.

my siblings and I

don't go digging with
questions anymore.

we create our own answers
through our mother's silence.

v.
but I, afraid,
beg for language
to let go the fear
of becoming
and hold
what too

will go.

OF BREATH

we were the kids
not allowed to go
near the water.
by the time
we were allowed

we were too big
for the pool
too big
to be swallowed whole.

my mother's fear of going
under has everything
to do with breath
the fear of
losing it.

when
the water's sting
paralyzes you
after your scream
is unheard.

when one
is unable to
come out
you swallow

each gulp

a punch
a grip at your throat
and your body is taken.

my mom was for none of it.

still
the summer
we forgot our dad,
there was a day

she went in the water,
a wave came,
she did not
mention learning

to swim.
a wave came,
she did not
mention drowning.

a wave,
her eyes were wide
waist deep
in her biggest fear.

i can't tell you
how long
we held hands,
how i realized
we were no longer

running,

planting our feet,
toes curling
and uncurling
in the sand,

daring the biggest wave to come.

OBLIGATION

It was in Kanifing that my parents met.

I imagine a big gust of wind.
All that sand clearing.

It is then that my father saw my mother's shadow,
confused by how the sun followed only her.

Her silhouette, a guiding force.

It was that shape,
that led him to my grandfather's compound.
To ask her to leave. To come to America.

Years ago, during the slamming of doors,
the physical altercations, my siblings' tears,
the constant screaming,

I would tell you that
my mother was only saying no to everything
that made her feel broken.

She was choosing her mental health.

Saying no to what made her crawl out of her body
in search of a new home.

No one was going to make her to say yes.

All that maternal training forgotten.

She was a person before she was a woman.

She was whole before she was a part of everybody.

Before everybody had a part of her.

She would say
I didn't kick him out.

I didn't tell your dad to leave.
He did that on his own.

I want to tell her that the truth is a much better story.
But I know better than to imply a choice
she was told to never make for herself.

So when my mother said she'd kill herself after I said
I'm moving out,
Munna was the first person I told.

She never wastes our time planning what to say.

She doesn't offer impossible solutions like

write her a letter,

tell her you're depressed,

tell her you don't want to belong here just to belong to someone else.

Leave. Leave. Leave!
Tell her you want love, the kind that doesn't keep you.

Instead, Munna asks, *What about your siblings?*
A question for my mother, but the one I always answer to.

Daughters of women from the continent know
we have a shared responsibility to the home.

Somehow, we are mothers, too, or in constant preparation of.

We know that love isn't about what you say yes to.

It is about what you stay for.

I've seen it when Uncle Yahya died.
How Mom put all our resources into his children,
his grave,
his garden,
and we continued to empty our stomachs.

How when I said I would leave,
my back ached.
I went outside ready to call for help to carry the load.

Then my mother called my phone and said, *mbe sunkarow kono. Yay hako*
tuen nye.
We're in the month of fasting, leave your forgiveness for me.

Spineless in my response, I cried.
I told myself, *just a few more steps.*

But sometimes, we encourage ourselves towards nothing.
We push past our limits to a point where we don't have ourselves.

We don't even care for what really happened.

PREP

nin ko kilin, eko fula. nin ko saba, eko naani.
when I say one, you say two. when I say three,
you say four. but your grandma? mbota tella.
I came from her. I don't get tired either.

My little body and quick tongue would walk away.
I should have known better. Most proverbs are
warnings, for the quick backhand or the first pop
at the mouth. It is the discovery of what you
should know. When that belt came? She
did not tire. I was out of breath. Wondering
from whom she gets hers.

You always ask the questions I can't answer
Fatima! Your grandma couldn't think about
things like age. She was 14 maaaybe maybe,
when the house caught fire. During that time,
what is age? My grandma told my mom to
take her brother and go. She died in the fire.
I told you that. They only knew it was her
'cause of the gold. Her jewelry, you know
Africans and their gold. So no matter what age,
you lost your mother. What else is there to keep
track of?

The first three of my grandmother's kids, each
after 8 months knew there couldn't be
anywhere safer than her womb. They left before
their bodies could touch the ground. The two

17

after, not older than 10, left for the sky on the
same day, only hours apart. The four after that,
*she says she doesn't remember but I know a lot
of them were sick.* The last one stayed long
enough to become the first to turn her into a
grandma. There's a lot to remember. A lot of
bodies gone, so many that don't get to speak.
So many stories about the woman whose being
brought me.

*I'm ready to go back and breathe the good air!
you guys don't even remember your first trip to
Gambia. How excited your grandma was? I'll
never forget the way she hugged your brother
and took you from my arms.*

I don't remember the first time I met my
grandmother. I remember before the second
time thinking there's no way this woman exists.
We must think we know where to find her.
This woman who's lost so much must be lost too.

*Don't cry, soon you will get used to her. Her mouth,
I know. Scared you? It's not really orange like that.
We came while she was having her snack. Curuwo
ya nyiwo baay tinya. The cola nut ruined her teeth.*

When the myth proved to be anything but,
I froze. I stared. She stood tall. Arms outstretched.
Mouth ablaze. Gold, all on her wrist.

ANEW

The blackest thing was us, the red was everything else.
None of it was beautiful.

He told me I was the most beautiful thing. Every time.
I said yes, every time.

It hurt every time, how I said yes to survive.
For what? For something so out of body, I began to see spirits.

Spirits who didn't know any better said *baby, this how men are.*
Some said *the love is hard before it's better.*

But none of them got to see better.
And I could no longer take this conditioning.

I wanted a red that was as beautiful as he said I was.
Then made him a red that made me feel like the sunset.

Besides, he tried to make a ghost of me first.

SANNO

Look! The beauty of the waves.

I close my eyes and cringe to hear the death in each crash.

Feel the sand, enjoy the shore.

I only feel my blood thinning. Desperate to jump in search of some kind of beginning.

An element so malleable some had to survive the wreckage!

Yes.

If you wanted to find the ones that have floated to shore, the survivors, all around there are plenty of other bodies that shine like mine.

WITH TIME

Only Godless children are this empty.

She says that it's just a jinn latching on

instead of a shadow,

too stuck in tradition to see me but

attempts to cuddle up under the earth

Maybe if I prayed more I'd have a body

for these creatures to hide in.

when did I become Godless in

attempts to find a beginning?

I know I'm late responding, but just wanted to say I miss and love you! Hope you've been well.

I know you all mean well

but to hear *I love you,*

when it does not sound believable

hurts. I don't feel the love,

I don't mean to come off ungrateful

hearing *how can I help?*

when a way out is more appealing,

it only stalls.

Nothing is comparable to a violence that's invisible and killing everything around it.

I know I deserve a better feeling.

I stink and

when I do get up

I'm walking with dead things

Everything is decomposing

in my bed all day

can you imagine?

waiting to be one of them.

21

Only Godless children are this empty.

I'm not suicidal.
Some days, I'm really fucking happy.
On the days that I'm not,
Language fails me.

I'm not suicidal.
I do think of the grave often.
How tight it might be,
even without a casket.
The white my family will drape my cold body in.
The only light I take with me.
The attempt at warmth.
The prayers my mother wishes I had memorized
in time to take with me.

As if God will ask me to recite ayat al-kursi.
God's power is one I will forever believe in.
It is not a power I doubt.
I just believe there is work I must do to recieve.

Labor that my body is resisting.
Labor my brain has no receptors to.

I'm not suicidal.

I just
have
no
grip.

REPETITION

We wake and in front of a mirror, we stand
just to walk away making no amends,

       but we always come back and try to amend.
       Mom's the best, being exactly who she is

and I choose to be exactly who I is.
She taught, I learned. We understand different.

       Two different countries, we move different.
       From where did you come, child? she asks.

Always the questions that aren't really asked.
From a woman whose body rejects this land.

       I scream that I didn't choose this landing.
       She screams that this land did not make me.

So I wait for her to recognize me.
We wake and in front of a mirror, we stand.

CHOICE

Look at us, built for the battle
but meant for
better and beyond.

They'll make a girl, view her body like a corpse
so that when her bones go back to the dirt
we say
she wanted to be there.

But the ground does not swallow
a body for foreplay, for power, for ownership,

but because it was put there.

INSTEAD OF MOURNING

Grief is a much gentler word.
But not one that could
represent this lamentation.

I don't know how to accept
the changing seasons,
and how nothing
comes back the same,
if it comes back at all.

Love requires a body to lend itself to.
Everything here is either dead drowning
or dying.

Here I am, begging and holding on
when I should be in search of someplace warm.

And if not for someone, then at least for myself.

EROSION

I lost count,
the days I stared out the window
thinking of ways to let go
this throbbing
in my chest.

Lost count,
how many times I tried to fill
the hollow
in the pit of my stomach.

I miss my grandmother.

In last night's dream,
the earth
rumbles.

Hard enough
for her remains
to move with
the land.

Fast
quick
and purposeful,
in the direction of the sea.

The plates diverge,
spread

and welcome her bones.

Then crushed
all in
that mid-atlantic ridge.
My grandmother
is no longer
one who has met her end
but who has gone back to the beginning.

Till she is the seabed.
Till she is the land kicked back
to the surface.

Till she is a road full of shells
my great, great, great
granddaughter is trying to pick
out.

REVOLUTION OF THE SCAVENGERS

HENNEH KYEREH KWAKU

This is a work of fiction. All names, characters, places, and incidents are a product of the author's imagination. Any resemblance to real events or persons, living or dead, is entirely coincidental.

Published by Akashic Books
©2020 Henneh Kyereh Kwaku

ISBN: 978-1-61775-887-4

Akashic Books
Brooklyn, New York, USA
Twitter: @AkashicBooks
Facebook: AkashicBooks
E-mail: info@akashicbooks.com
Website: www.akashicbooks.com

African Poetry Book Fund
Prairie Schooner
University of Nebraska
110 Andrews Hall
Lincoln, Nebraska 68588

live . . .

for those gone—
through the *bads*
& the floods

for those we pray
not to go
& those who offer the prayers

. . . *live*

poems will not return
you, here—but
they keep you alive, here

TABLE OF CONTENTS

PREFACE
by Henk Rossouw

Images of water run throughout Henneh Kyereh Kwaku's stunning and incisive series of prose poems, *Revolution of the Scavengers*. These images oscillate between water as the source of the speaker's despair—its scarcity in Hohoe, its overabundance in Accra—and water as the source of life itself: "As a child, I loved to jump & run in the rain—we had nothing to boast of but joy," Kwaku writes in "The Fear of a Thing Is the Beginning of a Search," using the kinetic rhythms that often enliven his work. To have nothing to boast of but joy speaks of the resilience evident in these poems, the sense that the creation of art offers a sanctuary, a place for questions, hopes, and dreams—defined as *tokonoma* by the Cuban poet José Lezama Lima.

Through the reimagining of the world that art enacts, the reimagining of circumstances, Kwaku's speaker in *Revolution of the Scavengers* withstands drowning in the contradictions of Ghana, contradictions that these poems elucidate and call to account. Occasionally the creativity entailed is as simple as the resourcefulness that the speaker remembers from his childhood—"Sometimes we used buckets to fetch the water dripping through our ceiling."

Water becomes the means by which Kwaku interrogates the impact of political corruption and global warming, twin issues that lead to water shortages, flood damage, and loss of life. Kwaku's work brings us enduring questions, refracted through the interiority of the speaker, about the state of contemporary Ghana—the emblematic postcolonial country, the home of Black Star Square, and the first nation on the African continent to gain its freedom from Great Britain. Few questions, animated by the postcolonial condition and its harsh disappointments, are as piercing as those at the heart of Kwaku's poem "Kutsiami":

The floods may come as they please & take us away. There are no ferrymen on floods. Will we ever get to the other side? The sons & daughters gone, where have they gone to? There are no ferrymen on floods. Death's linguist, will you hear us if we come bloating—floating—on water?

In a subtle pattern, the poems often end in questions about God or the Gods.

Kwaku takes great care to ground his sonic deftness and strong imagery in the daily concerns and conditions of everyday Ghanaians. Implicit, communal questions like, *Why? How could this happen? Who is responsible?* underwrite the matter-of-fact sentences that anchor the poems. In "Something Is in the Water," Kwaku writes, "The ground in Hohoe leaks water, the PVC pipes behind the Police HQ leak water—in Hohoe, water is scarce." The speaker's refreshing honesty evades the trap of complicit, state-sanctioned, post-liberation sentimentality: "If I do not fill my barrels on Monday, I'll have no water, no water till Thursday & this isn't a metaphor—Monday isn't about the beginning of this country & Thursday isn't how far we've come."

At the same time, the contradictions of contemporary Ghana include moments of fierce beauty, moments visible from the open window, moments of stillness, moments owed to fellow citizens passing by, as in "Abracadabra (An Empty Ark Is No Different from No Ark)": "Today, the cocks are crowing after the rains. This is Hohoe. The woman who sells *pito* by my window has fetched four barrels of water—she joins the cocks in praise of the God of rain." In Kwaku's poem, the woman's joy at the bounty of "four barrels of water" is an act of resistance, and the authority with which Kwaku's speaker utters, "This is Hohoe" is nothing less than the authority of love. Kwaku again marvels at everyday life and finds comfort in the presence of others in "Whatever Makes Us Laugh Isn't a Joke": "From my window, the town is alive again. Hohoe is alive. A woman packs crates of Coke in front of her shop, another woman sitting in front of her house, chest bare, shuffles her hair."

The poems in *Revolution of the Scavengers* are deeply invested in the love of a citizen for fellow citizens, citizens risking their all to stay alive—whether in Hohoe at its driest or in Accra when it floods, almost every year now. The speaker's love for the body politic gives rise to the despair and rage in his poems: "The dove will return, with a flower in the beak & people, bloating—floating—on water." The democratic care evident in the work of Henneh Kyereh Kwaku provides hope.

SOMETHING IS IN THE WATER

The PVC pipes are burst, from my condo I can see the water squirting out of the cracks. I know everything is cracked here, our roads, our laws, our schools—our lives. Everything is leaking just like the water squirts into the dirty gutter. The water becomes useless, these are not metaphors. The ground in Hohoe leaks water, the PVC pipes behind the Police HQ leak water—in Hohoe, water is scarce. If I do not fill my barrels on Monday, I'll have no water, no water till Thursday & this isn't a metaphor—Monday isn't about the beginning of this country & Thursday isn't how far we've come. Monday isn't Kwame Nkrumah & Thursday isn't Nana Addo. I know the pipes are burst, just like the police & their wives & husbands & kids, but who cares—who cares about this country where there is no God of accountability?

EVEN IN OUR DIFFERENCES THERE'S A SIMILARITY

Do not say my language fails & do not say it is primitive. They say sweat too is water, with different names. Like Accra & Hohoe, both Ghanaian towns but different names. The sun is great here but only produces waste water. PDS has been tweeting about where there'll be power cuts next. Thank God We're Not A Nigerians, said the FoKN Bois. Nigeria & Ghana, sweat & water. Someone says the difference between Ghana's economy & Nigeria's is Buhari. I think of an equal sign, I think of the subtraction sign—I drift back to Drobo when I was taught these signs but never understood. I still don't understand why Ghana & Nigeria do not add up. *Sweat too na water abi?* Let the Chinese come for the bauxite at Atiwa & show us how to fetch sweat for distillation. *Na only sweat we dey get from the sun o, but we shun the solar energy. Or sweat be wonna solar energy?* Ra, we know—the God of the sun. But who is the God of solar energy? & where's Ghana's God of the sun?

MOURNING MY COUNTRY

The streets of Hohoe do not flood, but the streets of Accra do. There are no lights on the Tema Motorway, but the streets of Hohoe are bright. In the night I mourn this country so I put off all my lights. If I ever get to know how to photograph the shadow of palm fronds on my wall, it may sell for a billion dollars someday & hang in a gallery somewhere—where somewhere is not Ghana. I pray there's water everyday so the palm tree does not die, before I discover how to capture this image. I pray we do not perish of thirst or corruption before we discover how to be free from this ailment. We prayed for the cedi, it still begs the dollar. Maybe America prays more than us or maybe there are more American Christians than there are Ghanaians. What do we say to the God of numbers? More water!

ANYTHING FOR THE BOYS?

January 2019 has come & gone like the Ghanaian presidential term, like the Accra floods. & like the floods, January took 190 lives through road accidents. I do not want to say the roads are bad anymore—the *bads* are *roads*. Do not say potholes, say manholes. Do not say reckless drivers—blame those who ask: *anything for the boys?* Do not blame because I've said so. Do not take yourself from the action & say: *they took GH₵ 1.00 from me.* Say: *I bribed the police.* Blame yourself. Do not say our flag does not dance when between the French & the American flag—our flag is cotton & shy, not just anything blows it away—so was this country made. This is your country. Our flag is not on any missile meant to wipe half of the world—our presidents are not Thanos to snap & wipe. We'd rather snap & get Noah's Ark for Accra before the floods.

IN THIS MINE, WE PRAY

Is it xenophobic to protect my water from Chinese miners? Galamseyers? It is not the Chinese we should fear or pray our anger on—it is he who brought them. Nobody asks the question. You see, in the quest to blame, we do not ask the right questions. We only point our index finger to the way of the blamed. We do not see the glass so we throw stones, when they break—we say no one told us. We are not the Graeae whose eye has been thrown into the black pot of human flesh. Do not take their lives—say to *Asaase Yaa:* let them not stand this ground, let them not break this ground. Say to *Maame Wata &* the River Goddesses: drown their axes, drown their shovels; sink their excavators. & to the God of the sky—*Nana Nyame*: let them be drunk on their sweat—let the sun beat them & save our waters.

THE FEAR OF A THING IS THE BEGINNING OF A SEARCH

As a child, I loved to jump & run in the rain—we had nothing to boast of but joy. I loved to walk in the rain, I learned to cry in the rain so no one sees my tears. It isn't that bad if you can boast of people, of joy. Father & mother had us—we had them. Sometimes we used buckets to fetch the water dripping through our ceiling. In Hohoe, the rain enters my room through the windows, I love the cool breeze of the rain but not the water in the room. I still do not mourn when it rains—I mourn when it is cloudy in Accra, I know someone is about to go—I know someone is about to be homeless. I want to imagine the silence after rains in Accra, fear brings silence—fear for the loss of the loved. Fear brings chaos too, fear for the loved, fear brings wailing—fear in search of the lost. I want to know if Ghana has a God of rain, of water, of flood? Is it *Ototrobonsu?* Is he related to the God of love or the God of death?

ABRACADABRA (AN EMPTY ARK IS NO DIFFERENT FROM NO ARK)

Today, the cocks are crowing after the rains. This is Hohoe. The woman who sells *pito* by my window has fetched four barrels of water—she joins the cocks in praise of the God of rain. I do not make a sound. I play music, I play a dirge instead. I pray a dirge. I try to write a poem for the lives lost but I fail. I say *Abracadabra* & whisper a wish, nothing happens. The Gods here do not respond to *Abracadabra*. Water is not good when it comes to kill. Water is not good if there's no Ark: I do not blame the water, I do not blame the Gods—if the Ark comes, it'd leave empty. The dove will return, with a flower in the beak & people, bloating—floating—on water.

WHATEVER MAKES US LAUGH ISN'T A JOKE

From my window, the town is alive again. Hohoe is alive. A woman packs crates of Coke in front of her shop, another woman sitting in front of her house, chest bare, shuffles her hair. An eagle flies across, no I don't know what bird it is, in English— eagle or hawk. *Ɔkɔdie,* not *Akorɔma.* The mountains are foggy. The weather app says it is cloudy & yes it is. At least it tells it as it is, I'm disappointed it can't tell the names of those who'll be gone if it rains in Accra. There's an 80% chance of precipitation in Accra & same percentage of at least 5 deaths in Accra & same percentage of people missing in Accra after the flood. The app didn't say this. A man tweets: Ghana is a joke. No, a joke is supposed to be funny, this isn't. Deaths aren't funny. Corruption isn't funny. Nothing is funny. Whatever makes us laugh isn't the joke. Do not pray for jokes, there's no God of jokes.

WELCOMING A GHANAIAN GOD

It is raining in Accra, so I stay away from the news. Hohoe is fine, the children are enjoying the rain, playing. The adults are indoors. You can't do this in Accra, your child will be gone before your first moan. About a month ago, Kofi Kingston became WWE's first African-born world champion, his mother says he's a full Ghanaian. Not African-American. Not Ghanaian-American—he's not hyphenated. He's full. She makes me believe again that being Ghanaian is something to be proud of. About a month ago, a Ghanaian comedian makes a terrorist scene somewhere in America, CIA invites him, no, they pick him up. Imagine a joke putting you on the same pedestal as ISIS or Osama or Sadam. Ghanaians roast the comedian on Twitter, Ghanaians embrace Kofi everywhere. Kofi comes to Ghana at a time it is raining, flooding, people bloating—floating—on water. Has our God arrived to save us? From the floods? If Kofi is our God, then he has failed—there's a woman in Hohoe who doesn't know Kofi.

KUTSIAMI

Kutsiami the benevolent boatman;
when I come to the river shore
please ferry me across
I do not have tied in my cloth-end
the price of your stewardship.

—Kofi Awoonor, "The Journey Beyond"

Let us make jokes of our presidents when they falter. Let us laugh, *my brothers &*
sisters for today we are, tomorrow unknown. The floods may come as they please &
take us away. There are no ferrymen on floods. Will we ever get to the other side?
The sons & daughters gone, where have they gone to? There are no ferrymen on
floods. Death's linguist, will you hear us if we come bloating—floating—on water?
Will you carry us into the chamber where we'd be made ancestors? Kutsiami, will
you ferry us home? Kutsiami, I hear your praise, I hear of your diplomacy—we
come before thee—with knees bent & incense burning—do tell the God of the
flood to close the gates, we have seen our folly rise like the rubbish we dump into
the gutters & waters. Save us.

NOAH

The footbridge. The footbridge is a home to the homeless, under the footbridge is a home to the homeless. In the news, a church opens its gates to the homeless to sleep overnight. But that church is not in Ghana. The weather is good for a good sleep but someone prays it doesn't rain. I imagine the water, the floods washing people away like debris. I fear. I open my eyes. I cry. Over here, Noah is all of us—stubborn—he doesn't hear a thing. Even after the dream, he says there'll be no flood. It is raining. The bridges are floating. I dream & I see people bloating—floating—on water. Now I pray: *Lord, let this be far from us.*

A FIREBALL SCREAMS

Ghana Web reports, Modern Ghana reports, other local news outlets report—we believe but we want confirmation—BBC, Al Jazeera & CNN. Al Jazeera reports— *Gas depot blasts kill at least seven in Accra.* The video circulating on WhatsApp & other social media passes for a bombing scene in any America versus Iraq movie as a fireball umbrellas the city. Edvard Munch's the scream has no voice but a body yet we hear the scream—mysterious. In the video we hear the scream but no bodies—which means lives are leaving bodies, which means bodies are becoming ashes, which means people are being roasted—people are roasting the kebab seller for lighting the match, (the kebab seller didn't leak the gas or plant the gas station in the middle of the city)—but he doesn't use human bodies for kebab. I cannot blame, I cannot question the Gods. Which of the Gods? The God of fire or the God of fuel stations? A few people roast the government. We are the people & we're the tribes & we're the government. Maybe we should roast ourselves for not knowing the laws & for knowing the laws & entombing them in dead ears.

NEVER AGAIN

3rd June, 2016—a year after June 3, 2015 & the headlines read—*1st Anniversary of June 3 disaster, how it happened; lessons learned.* The land choruses—*never again*—but we lie. We're tribes of forgetful people. The only things we remember are where our borders lie—& even that, we forget & we fight to remember. In the headlines, they say—*lessons learned*—but I swear no lessons have been learned. The only lessons may be—*after disaster, there's money in the pockets of a few as we mourn*—souls gone with the wind. Some bodies not found, some bodies found—but not seen. These are not just bodies, these are brothers & sisters & fathers & mothers & children & cousins & families & teachers & doctors & security personnel & filling station attendants & presidents of the future & pastors & the greats-to-come & whole tribes carried in one & people, the people of this land gone through fire & water & they cannot become ancestors because ancestors do not die through fire & water. No lessons learned, no lessons learned. We await the next, to celebrate, the next to celebrate the next.

MURDER IN THE CREEK

2076 people did not die. 2076 were killed. 2076 were murdered. They were killed through bad roads & poor driving skills. & through people who shouldn't be driving but are driving because there's no one to stop them. 2076 killed, children have been made orphans through the murder of 2076. Through lawlessness. Through incompetence. Some children will be made what the society hates to make through the murder of 2076. Politics has killed 2076, 2076 people, 2076 bloods, whole families killed within 2076. Mothers killed, fathers killed, brothers murdered, sisters murdered. Everybody killed & nobody does a thing about it. Everybody saw 2076 murdered & nobody stopped the murderer. 2076 is bigger than 2017. & 2076 people of this land were murdered in 2017 through road accidents. All killed. All murdered.

REVOLUTION OF THE SCAVENGERS

My son, I had it in my heart to build a house for the Name of the Lord my God.
                                         —King David (1 *Chronicles* 22:7)

*Ghana Web, News Headline: Gov't begins demolition of Judges' bungalows for National
Cathedral.* & the prophet(s) agreed that David builds a temple in the name of the
Lord. But can a man build a house for the Lord when the Lord has not asked?
There's a stale smell of—*a national temple, a national cathedral, needful, not needful?*—
in the atmosphere & as the nation reasoned, the Lord spoke to the prophet(s)—
*your hands are bloody, man . . . don't build a thing in my name with those bloody hands,
man*—now, the prophet(s) asked the King—*are your hands free of blood?* The floods
have come to take the bloods in your name. The *bads* have taken bloods in your
name. They come with your hands & leave with your hands. Your fingerprints are
all over these graveyards. Bloody hands build no temples, my Lord—so the King
built no temples. & this was a wise King who loved his people.

25

LAZY YOUTH

This nation is a vehicle without headlights—walking through a dark tunnel, everyone thinks the end of the tunnel is bright—but nobody is right or wrong because nobody has been at the end. This nation is a car without *trafgators** (—a metaphor my friends know me for)—nobody knows the turn it is taking or nobody is prepared for whatever turn it takes or about to take. A nation says—*argh! These youth are lazy, these youth are anything but good*—but nobody prepared these youth for this life of this nation that they're supposed to fit in. Who failed? Who's anything but good? This nation is a nation of faith, walks by faith—blind faith. Is that the fate of this nation? This nation has never given up. We cry again: *Lord, you have sent us the rains for our farms & so we do not thirst—& the roads so we shall pass even through the red sea—do not send Noah, send the ship else we die. Our faith stinks & our fate is sinking.*

trafgators: traffic indicators

ACKNOWLEDGMENTS

"Something Is in the Water," "Mourning My Country," "The Fear of a Thing Is the Beginning of a Search," "Abracadabra (An Empty Ark Is No Different from No Ark)," and "Whatever Makes Us Laugh Isn't a Joke" originally appeared in *Tupelo Quarterly*, Issue 19.

"Anything for the Boys?" originally appeared in *Tampered Press*, Issue 3.

TRY KISSING GOD
AFUA ANSONG

Published by Akashic Books
©2020 Afua Ansong

ISBN: 978-1-61775-883-6

Akashic Books
Brooklyn, New York, USA
Twitter: @AkashicBooks
Facebook: AkashicBooks
E-mail: info@akashicbooks.com
Website: www.akashicbooks.com

African Poetry Book Fund
Prairie Schooner
University of Nebraska
110 Andrews Hall
Lincoln, Nebraska 68588

TABLE OF CONTENTS

PREFACE
by Romeo Oriogun

The first time I saw Akan symbols was on the foreheads of some masks hawked by a man on Labadi Beach in Accra. The symbols felt like maps pointing the way to the past, telling stories that must not be forgotten. This is what Afua Ansong's *Try Kissing God* has done. She has taken these symbols and woven them into folktales, into poems that interrogate the place of women in Ghanaian society, and into poems that are searching for a way back home from the diaspora. Yet these poems are not just interested in history and in the past; they are alive, present, and urgent. In "GYE NYAME: Except for God/if not for God" Ansong writes:

> Nyame wears
> a strange mouth.
>
> It is like small rocks
> with oceans running
>
> inside them. Touch,
> and you may
>
> shatter into eternal
> mortality.

The poem asks us not to be afraid to seek our mortality. What is the search for life if not a search for home? Is the search for a place to belong not a part of our eternal struggle? Ansong knows that the search for home doesn't stop. She also knows the importance of names in the search for home. People have spent time searching for names that will become faces, long-lost families, home—but what happens when your name is a stranger?

Ansong ponders these questions and asks in her poem, "SANKƆFA: Go back for it/return for it":

> You were not even named after a tree
>
> giving solace to the sacrificial goat.
> So how would they know where
> to return you when the thing
> that loves you calls you home?

One should not make the mistake of assuming that Ansong is a stranger to her home. On the contrary, in these poems she leads us to her roots. She assuredly walks through the doors into the history of her people. She knows the rewards of looking into the mirror and seeing on her face the sweetness of knowing home. In her poem "NYAME DUA: Tree of God/ God's altar," she writes:

> Woman knows the sweetest part of tree
> is hidden between Asase Yaa's thighs:
> a treasure for the brave who will dig
> in or the tired who will chance upon
> the roots where she keeps deliverance.

Whether this home is the celebration of a king, or the way people who are mentally ill and people who are homeless are treated, Ansong is not afraid of it. She wants us to see all sides of societies that reflect the beauty of history and our everyday reality. In doing so, she's giving us the privilege of seeing the diversity and the struggle of others in our everyday lives. She's helping us become a people filled with love, because we can only begin to love the world when we realize what is beyond us.

I am fascinated by these poems, and I am grateful that a poet like Afua

Ansong exists in our world today. She is skillful and deliberate with her use of language—she knows the traps, and she knows how to confront them without falling prey to them. She wants us to see what she sees; she also wants us to see how in history and in the present, the bodies of women are at war, and we are often silent. In the tradition of a long line of female poets, she reaches into history to show us that, because mankind hasn't been held accountable, the war on the bodies of women is still raging. Ansong urges us not to be passive witnesses, to make home a safer place. In "FI-HANKRA: Safe compound house," she writes:

> You should have said something—more than
> *he'll stop* when Maa Naa told you her brother
> would climb on her, in the night;
> the room lit by the cleanness of his eyes
> and the smell of guilt staining her nose
> through the darkness.

In her quest to bring these Akan symbols into poetry, Ansong knows she's also moving toward home, whether through her natural hair or the sound of a drum. She is aware of her journey, and she is saying to a large of number of Africans, *You are not alone, I too have been there, I am there.*

The poetry of Afua Ansong is a gift to us. She belongs to a tradition of Ghanaian poets that are rooted in the African soil—poets such as Ama Ata Aidoo, Kojo Laing, Abena Busia, and Kofi Awoonor, who weave history, its images, folktales, and symbols into their poetry. Afua Ansong's poetry is a walk through history, and in these poems she is a griot, singing to us of things we've lost. We are, she sings, lucky to be alive at a time like this, and we are blessed and lifted into her poems as she leads us. We are privileged to be on this journey with her. We are walking home.

Adinkra in Twi, an Akan language, means farewell. Initially stamped onto funeral cloths and used to communicate with the spirit world (mourners wore the cloths for a year before washing them), *Adinkra* is now fashioned into decorations, art on buildings, logos, jewelry, and tattoos. The sixty-plus symbols, several of which have variations, carry individual messages as phrases or proverbs describing the norms of the Akans. The symbols included here have been excavated from nineteenth-century documents, arts, and ruins.

SANKƆFA
GO BACK FOR IT/RETURN FOR IT

In the naming of things after things
you are named after no one;
not the red-eyed crab or the shooting gun.

Your sister carries her ancestors' names
the way a fighter carries praise for war.

She is named after the living and the dead.
She is the afterlife and you are the present.

When she raises her lower lip so high
it almost touches her nose, you see

your grandmother and your aunt and her.
Others see it too and say how you don't take

her face but how you stole the ears and chin
of your mother. At least your large forehead

belongs to you, or was it a gift of excess clay?
You were not even named after a tree

giving solace to the sacrificial goat.
So how would they know where
to return you when the thing
that loves you calls you home?

ADINKRAHENE
KING OF THE ADINKRA SYMBOLS

In the dream, you are God. Ink and water worship you.
The spines of shapes offer themselves as sacrifice
to your imagination. You drink in and thirst
no more. Your hands are tied to your back.

In the dream, you are wet. Splashes of ink drip
from your right hand. You sit on the cold floor
with your feet sinking into a rock.

In the dream, you lie on brown grass to wail.
Thick drops of ink fall to your face:
not like dew, but as though someone else
were at a loss—your wife or children—inheriting
your sorrow. You dip your fingers into your jaws
to draw shapes on a white slate.

In the dream, you are the red tree bark cut into pieces
by a farmer and cooked in a cauldron, high heat,
with borrowed water. You bubble and overflow.
When the sun sets, you cool.

In the dream, you are a calabash carved
into the shape of a vase. The humans pour
something into you, thick and fiery.
They leave a bat at the curl
of your lips and it drinks until you are empty.

NYAME DUA
TREE OF GOD/GOD'S ALTAR

Nyame, not in the habit of gardening,
leaves his tree to Asase Yaa to tend
which means ants biting bark, deer licking
sap and woman searching for seeds,

which means woman loving tree,
making friends with tree,
pulling apart flowers and branches
to build an altar for Nyame.

Woman knows the sweetest part of tree
is hidden between Asase Yaa's thighs:
a treasure for the brave who will dig
in or the tired who will chance upon
the roots where she keeps deliverance.

When the seeds shudder at dawn,
it is only woman who sees
what Asase Yaa can do with her mouth.

BOA ME NA ME MMOA WO
HELP ME SO I CAN HELP YOU

You guard the market stores with your body
at night. It is a banquet for mosquitoes
that wrestle with coils and nets
and substance for the light Accra wind to toss.

The quick lips of the market women
kick you into a rising at dawn which responds
to labor but not light. Your heels wear cracks
from following men and women whose necks

stiffen and stick firm to the weight of this world.
What can you not carry? Dead or living;
a Christmas goat (whole or only its head
smelling of burnt skin.) Under your armpits

you hold a storm, a piercing stench
that reminds them you are human,
that for you water is sacred,
for your feet and face daily
but on your body weekly.

You are odd like the small vultures
making conversations with God
about how to grow hairs on their heads
and how to swallow tired things whole.

NYAME NTI
BECAUSE OF GOD . . .

On the occasion of your suicidal thoughts, you begged *Otwereduapong* to kill you, move you a little closer to the train tracks, pinch in your cheeks and suck blood from your ventricles, fasten the beat of your pulse, glue your eyelids—your hands quivered with knife in hand and jaws trembled with pills in throat—maybe a gunshot, strayed towards your chest, perhaps madness (or did you already possess this?)

You couldn't do it yourself. These same knees that prayed for glory now begged for murder.

But God refused to move. He wouldn't degrade himself to this pity party and if you were going to end your life, you had to put your own hands to use. *Otwereduapong* asked that you saw your coffin, felt the splinters of fine wood at your fingertips. Something about how it took great measures to make you and kiss you into life.

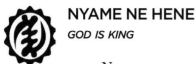

NYAME NE HENE
GOD IS KING

Nyame mmrane:
Ototrobonsu
Ɔbaatanpa
Ɔkatakyie
Ɔsaagyefo
Otwereduapong

This symbol was made for man
who at times, being able to make
children, sacrifice humans, drink
blood, enslave, set free, keep
servants' head bowed at his small
feet and marry many mouths,
think that he could power kingdoms
the way Nyame turned on the universe.

Someone has to answer to Nyame.
Nyame speaks for himself.

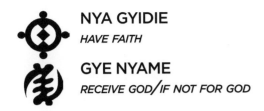

NYA GYIDIE
HAVE FAITH

GYE NYAME
RECEIVE GOD/IF NOT FOR GOD

Gye in Akan
suggests an offering;

to have someone
at the receiving end,

to desire to let go,
completely,

often assuming
trust exists

which is *Gyi*
die, which sounds

often like *Gye de*—
take and eat—

someone cooks
a meal, palatable or not,

boiled yams
with okro stew,

male crabs, cow hide,
perhaps, gives

it to you in a clean bowl,
food that may turn

your intestines outside in
or clean your red

throat. You lick your lips
and thank your tongue.

But how do you *take*
God—*Gye Nyame*

—unless they mean to say
except for God.

For Nyame cannot be chewed
on like the bones of a quail

or kept in the palm
like sweat.

PEMPAMSIE
SEW IN READINESS

Your grandmother's zealous effort to teach you how to sew forces a needle to your brown iris. She dealt more with dark cocoa grounds than indigo tie & dye cloth. When she wraps a Woodin cloth around herself, the folds of her arms flap down: a sight that embarrasses the holes on the surface of the moon. She, a good woman, did not need buttons to be undressed (or touched) by men. She stirred their spirits until they wept. Mercy.

Her mouth knows the hands that will light the match to hell. Red thunder. Fast. Grandma believes virgin brides who wrap *kente* around their oval bellies lay green eggs on their husband's square beds. They hum, sit, incubate yearnings so bright; the sun eclipsed begs to peek.

What you are good at, your mother and father's women, is turning fire under hot pans, grinding loud peppers into humble melodies; tamed tomatoes, pounding warm plantains and young cassavas in excellent rhythm; these ripe hands know the sweet flavors of War. Joy.

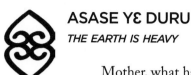

ASASE YƐ DURU
THE EARTH IS HEAVY

Mother, what have we done with earth's flower?
Forcing it into holes of the dead
and wrapping it around cold limbs
not to warm but to exchange for coins and grief.
We laugh with the white man who drags
our hands into the deep soil until we are hoes
turning the calm of earth.

This cotton pulls children out of our bellies
to chain their nakedness.
This cotton is the harvest of our fingers
we hide under our beds and uncover again
to weave dresses that cover the holes in our skin.
This cotton drives away our angels
and brings near spirits with rusted keys
to ring in our ears:

if you want to be free you can stop picking,
if you want to run, you can bury yourself,
lie in the field of flowers, white and soft, your burial,
until water pours out of your holes.

Mother, do not fear.
The earth itself will drink our blood.

TAMFO BƐBRƐ
THE ENEMY WILL SUFFER

In your dreams, the devil recites at the waist of a river.

His stanzas touch you. You eat his words and they almost choke you as you swallow. The words digest and you watch the talons of an eagle grow from your toenails. Somehow, fur sprouts on your face.

His lines pull you in closer to the currents but you beg, ask him to stop the incantations.

The devil retaliates with stronger verbs like shut / cage / spike / crack / rock and opens his glass wings. You see what this song has turned you into.

You push yourself into the currents, wake up gasping for air, yearning to hear the rest.

ƐPA
HANDCUFFS

You rehearse the lines until your gaze breaks the silence in the room:
To whom are you worthy, black woman? The sound of "woman" falls
like the metal clapper of a bell. In your mouth, your tongue is swollen
and all the words are bloody.

You try again but the voices say you are some borrowed property,
stolen golden goods: something they want to watch in a museum with blue walls.
You leave *worthy* and try for *free*, swing your hand until it pushes pressures of
possibilities.

Now you listen to your unborn children turn
as white hands trespass and knead your stomach.
To whom must you reveal your strength?

You quirk your head and tend to the wrinkles of your neck, murmur:
A black woman is a thawing lake in spring,
a porcupine hiding her quills from her children who surprise her protection,
or the open sky, translucent, bright, still full of rain.

DUAFE
WOODEN COMB

When you cut those loose permed strands off your head, what being could not call you African?

The doves turned their wings inside out to spare their eyes to this wonder, this woman thing, and the ants stopped sweet-talking, linked their arms together, sang to you, this woman thing.

Those golden peacock earrings revealed the wooden frame of your face, burned by the rich American sun. The buzzing of Nigel's blade taught your hair the lines to follow and forced a naked submission. At some point, your mother said you resembled the adowa dancers who pouted their small lips and hopped around the sand as if tackling a soccer ball from their ancestors.

The tragedy was in the pulling; the comb, like your four fingers running through your hair, only turned your eyes a pepper red. You can't count how many times you wished your hair waved blond—and with blond you don't mean dye, but a death to coil, a murder to the strands that refused to tame their taste for wildness.

When the mass asked *why did you cut your hair?* you had no answer. You must have dared to accept your face just the way it was made. The bliss of afros never reached your backyard to offer comfort or say *here is beauty, take it and wrap it around your head, own a haircut that divides your age into two.*

Blessed are those who bantu knot and oil massage their scalps to sleep and rise with coconut oil stains on their pillows.
Blessed are the naturals that plead with dandruffs after a co-wash.
Blessed are you who transition and possess the best of two worlds.
Blessed are those who cut and cut until they turn into their roots.

FIHANKRA
SAFE COMPOUND HOUSE

You should have said something—more than
he'll stop when Maa Naa told you her brother
would climb on her, in the night;
the room lit by the cleanness of his eyes
and the smell of guilt staining her nose
through the darkness. He forgot kinship
and redrew blood lines. It was your guilt perhaps
that made you admit that your body
also accused his hands of a similar sin. Perhaps
her defense for his disease ate at her gums,
left holes in her throat.

You should have asked,
you are asking now:
Maa Naa, were you afraid?

DONNO
DRUMS

At the artifacts show,
outdoors, you see a drum
and touch its face,
hit it right in the middle
where the leather tears.
The red tag says $35
but the man selling it sees
that you are drawn to it
and that you want to beat it,
carry it home with you in your red van
for times when you are on your bed
and see how the birds
dip their necks back to swallow
light. You take your hands off when he says
$20, you want to get it off my hands?
You don't look at his hands to see whether
he is responsible for the decay,
whether he understands that drumming
anything creates bruises,
like drumming the stomach of a woman
who is forced out of her country
or drumming a little boy who carries healing
in his arms. You raise the drum.
It wears small rings around its waist.

ƆDƆ NNYEW FIE KWAN
LOVE NEVER LOSES ITS WAY HOME

You whisper *home is a song to the womb*
into the green night, your slender fingers
arched around his wanting ears.
He tames your clay hands,
lowers your fingers into his and replies
still you must return to it.

In the sky, the children of heaven
keep still; not like the butterflies
that flutter their glory at day.
Now they cannot be seen.
He walks you (not with you
perhaps he is absent but still here)

to the bench in the open garden
where the moon sees his whiteness
and your darkness. You think of the sunrise,
what it will expose, and of his girlfriend
whose name, its tune rather, is stuck
to his earlobe. You rub it between
your index finger and thumb,
see if seven years can be fragile.

You wait, the moon, you and him
until the pink hidden light of day awakens.

GYE NYAME
EXCEPT FOR GOD/IF NOT FOR GOD

Nyame wears
a strange mouth.

It is like small rocks
with oceans running

inside them. Touch,
and you may

shatter into eternal
mortality. Not in the way

a baby's eyes closes
with her mouth over

her mother's nipples,
slightly ajar,

or how a beetle sheds
life and still lives

with straight wings.
This rock of mouth

is for Nyame to sing
orphaned creatures

through dull jaws
unto dry banks.

Nyame also has
a tongue that

remembers ways
to mourn the dying.

NOTES

According to myth, the Adinkrahene was created by Gyaman Adinkra, a king from Ivory Coast who was imprisoned in Ashanti land for blaspheming the golden stool.

Nyame is an Akan word for God.

Asase Yaa is the earth goddess of fertility.

BOA ME NA ME MMOA WO—"Help me so I can help you" is written after Kayaye, women who hustle in the market of Accra by carrying the loads of others.

The italicized list in "NYAME NE HENE" are mmrane, also known as accolades or praise.

NYA GYIDIE—"Have faith" & GYE NYAME—"Receive God/if not for God": Gye in Akan means take (to receive) while Gyi can mean except or if not. The word for trust, believe and faith in Akan is Gyi Die.

ASASE YƐ DURU—"the earth is heavy": Nsa'a is money collected from family members and friends to help cover the cost of burying one's dead. Asawa is cotton inserted into the nostrils of the dead and wrapped around their bodies to absorb fluids.

ACKNOWLEDGMENTS

I am grateful to the editors of *The Rumpus* and *Wraparound South* for publishing the poems Fihankra and Duafe respectively.

I am also grateful to Susan Merrel, Julie Sheehan and the team at The Watermill Center, NY for housing me as I wrote this manuscript. Special thanks to Kelly Dennis who read a first draft of this manuscript.

Thanks to Kathleen Davis at the University of Rhode Island (GSEG) for supporting me with grants for further research.

Thanks to Kwame Dawes, who has encouraged my journey, Chris Abani, and Ashley Strosnider for your patience with my manuscript.

Finally, I am grateful to my family, especially M'afia, who I called often to discuss the meaning of these symbols. And of course Nyame, my favorite muse.